PRAISE FOR *THEY SPOKE OF ME*

"How did the apostles understand and preach about Jesus? How does the Old Testament relate to the New Testament? What is promised and what is fulfilled? Smith and Berry show how our Bible fits together, the Old and the New, promise and fulfillment, hope and its realization in Jesus Christ. This readable and energetic account will help anyone see how the Old Testament provides the scaffolding for the New Testament. Recommended for all serious students of the Bible."

Michael F. Bird, Lecturer in Theology at Ridley College in Melbourne, Australia; author of *Jesus the Eternal Son* and *The Gospel of the Lord*

"Most Christians I meet are unsure what to do with the Old Testament. They find it inaccessible and incomprehensible, so they spend their time in the New as much as possible. Brandon Smith and Everett Berry recognize that the New Testament comes to life in light of the Old. They have created a tool to help learners set aside their misgivings and see the Old Testament as a faithful witness to the person and work of Christ. Christians are a people of two testaments. *They Spoke of Me* seeks to help us open the storeroom of the entire Bible, bringing forth treasures both new and old."

Jen Wilkin, Bible teacher; author of *None Like Him* and *Women of the Word*

"Too often Jesus is understood apart from the Old Testament, but we forget that Jesus's person, ministry, and work cannot be grasped apart from the Bible's storyline. For this reason, Smith and Berry have done the church a great service by teaching us about Jesus from the Old Testament. If you want to know grow in your knowledge and devotion to Christ, this book is for you. It is a rich feast that I hope many will read and enjoy, inspiring the church to live faithfully for Christ Jesus our Lord."

Stephen J. Wellum, Professor of Christian Theology at The Southern Baptist Theological Seminary; author of *God the Son Incarnate* and *Kingdom through Covenant*

"In John Stott's classic book, *Between Two Worlds*, he argued that the key to effective preaching and teaching is not mastering certain *techniques*, but being mastered by certain *convictions*. Obviously, one conviction that must master us is that the Bible is God's Word. But what is the message of the Bible? To whom does it point? Drawing upon Luke 24 and several important Old Testament examples, Smith and Berry show us that the Hero of the Bible is Jesus. This little Christ-centered book can be used in a number of helpful ways: (1) as an introduction into the world of Christ-centered hermeneutics, (2) for personal Bible study (as it is quite devotional), or (3) as a commentary to consult when teaching on selected passages. I wholeheartedly recommend it."

Tony Merida, Lead Pastor of Imago Dei Church in Raleigh, NC; Associate Professor of Preaching at Southeastern Baptist Theological Seminary; author of *The Christ-Centered Expositor*

"Smith and Berry have served the church well in producing this accessible and readable book on biblical theology and typology. This is heart-warming and mind-stretching truth that will help both the newcomer and the old-timer navigate the depths of the riches of Christ and the Old Testament."

Liam Goligher, Senior Minister of Tenth Presbyterian Church in Philadelphia, PA; author of *The Jesus Gospel*

"The portrait of Jesus reflected in the story of the Old Testament is central for the life of the disciple, and *They Spoke of Me* displays this beautiful portrait for the follower of Jesus. The work unfolds several Old Testament vignettes, all of which demonstrate Jesus as both the key to the overarching narrative of Scripture and the key to God's redemptive plan from the beginning. Readers are invited, as those first followers on the road to Emmaus, to discover the beauty and power of Jesus foreshadowed in the Old Testament. Take up and read!"

Darian R. Lockett, Associate Professor of Biblical and Theological Studies at Talbot School of Theology; author of *Understanding Biblical Theology*

"Our goal as Christians is to be like Jesus. To do that, we need to know Jesus through the Spirit-inspired Scriptures, from Genesis to Revelation. Smith and Berry help us to do just that in *They Spoke of Me*. Accessible, engaging, and informative, this book will help the lay reader and the seminary professor alike see Jesus on every page of the Bible."

Matthew Y. Emerson, Chair of Religion at Oklahoma Baptist University; Executive Director of the Center for Baptist Renewal; author of *Christ and the New Creation* and *Between the Cross and the Throne*

THEY SPOKE OF ME

HOW JESUS UNLOCKS THE OLD TESTAMENT

BRANDON D. SMITH
AND EVERETT BERRY

They Spoke of Me: How Jesus Unlocks the Old Testament

© 2018 by Brandon D. Smith and Everett Berry
All rights reserved.

ISBN 978-1-948022-01-9

Rainer Publishing
www.RainerPublishing.com
Spring Hill, TN

Printed in the United States of America

All Scripture quotations have been taken from the Christian Standard Bible®, Copyright © 2018 by Holman Bible Publishers. Used by permission. Christian Standard Bible® and CSB® are federally registered trademarks of Holman Bible Publishers.

To Christa and Tabitha

CONTENTS

Acknowledgements 11
Foreword 13
Walking the Emmaus road 17
1 - Humanity 23
2 - Noah 43
3 - Melchizedek 61
4 - Moses 85
5 - Israel 107
6 - Davidic kings 133
7 - Temple 155
8 - Psalms 177
9 - Jonah 197
Returning to Emmaus 217
Recommended reading 225
Endnotes 227
About the authors 239

ACKNOWLEDGEMENTS

Writing a book is no small endeavor, and there are numerous people who have played an important role in this work. We're grateful, first and foremost, for our supportive wives and loving kids. They inspire us, encourage us, and sharpen us in ways we cannot quantify. Many thanks to Matthew Emerson, Patrick Schreiner, Russell Meek, and Jason Kees for their feedback on some of the earliest drafts. A special thank you to Criswell College for granting Everett a sabbatical to work on this book.

FOREWORD

One of the most encouraging signs of renewal in evangelicalism is the growing interest in biblical theology, particularly in tracing the story of the whole Bible. As evangelicals, we are well-known for our exegesis of individual paragraphs or verses on Sunday mornings. It isn't uncommon to hear about preachers who have spent years unpacking Matthew, John, or Romans to their congregations. Such an approach is to be celebrated in many ways since it reflects an intense desire to know God's Word deeply. On the other hand, more and more of our churches are limited by Sunday morning services, and thus if one spends ten years in Romans, it is possible that the only sermons a person hears for ten years are on Romans. Large swaths of the Bible are neglected and perhaps forgotten. We can imagine that some might get lost in the welter of details, with the result that the storyline of the Bible becomes rather hazy. We want our people to see the whole narrative, to know the big picture.

Brandon Smith and Everett Berry, in this important and accessible work, are part of the larger movement reclaiming biblical theology for the church. They don't just claim, however, to do biblical theology. They show that biblical theology rightly done is Christ-centered, that Jesus himself unlocks the story of the Old Testament (OT). In my experience, some OT scholars disagree. They interpret the OT only in its historical context and exclude the New Testament (NT) in interpreting the OT. At one level we can understand why, and such OT scholars are preserving something very important. The integrity of the OT itself is preserved by interpreting the books which make up the OT canon in their social and historical context. We all know of examples where the OT message is drowned out or submerged to a significant extent by a superficial appeal to the NT. If we don't reckon with the voice of OT authors in their own context, we aren't truly doing exegesis.

The concern for the historical context of the OT writings, however, should not be our only concern. As evangelicals, we believe that the canonical writings are inspired by God, that they represent not just a human voice, but a divine voice. I am not suggesting that the divine author contradicts the human author, but the divine author of the Scriptures brings out what was concealed in the OT from the beginning. The OT is a forward-looking book; it anticipates the fulfillment of divine promises and covenants made with Adam, Noah, Abraham, Moses, David, and the prophets. NT writers, then, perceive the fullness of what was in the OT writings all along. In other words, the OT helps us interpret the NT, and the NT helps us interpret the OT. Evangelical OT scholars who shear off the NT in their work actually contribute to a problem in evangelical pulpits. Pastors may neglect the OT since they wonder how it can apply to contemporary believers, and when they turn to some OT commentaries, even some commentaries by evangelicals, they find justification for their neglect of the OT since the discussion is almost exclusively historical.

This brings me back to Smith and Berry, for they rightly lay out the Christological character of the OT. Certainly, there is a superficial and thin way of reading Jesus out of the OT, but if there isn't a deep and thick connection between Jesus and the OT, questions are raised about whether the OT is truly part of the Christian canon. Indeed, questions are raised about how Jesus Christ is the fulfillment of the promises made in the OT. Thankfully, Smith and Berry give us a satisfying taste of how the message of the OT finds its key—its fulfillment—in Jesus Christ. There is always more to be said, but we can be thankful for books like this, which unpack for us what Jesus meant when he said, "If you believed Moses, you would believe me, because he wrote about me" (John 5:46 CSB).

Thomas R. Schreiner
Professor of New Testament Interpretation and Biblical Theology
The Southern Baptist Theological Seminary

WALKING THE EMMAUS ROAD

In Luke 24:13-35, we read of two disciples who were traveling from Jerusalem to a village called Emmaus. They were distraught over the recent death of Jesus the Nazarene, their Lord and master, who had been condemned to death and crucified by the Romans as a criminal. And now there were reports that Jesus had been raised from the dead.

These facts just did not fit together. This is why these Jewish pilgrims, one of them named Cleopas, were debating these matters with passion. They could not harmonize these events in their own minds. They were baffled by these events, yes, but even more—their understanding of the Old Testament (OT) did not coincide with what had just transpired. The sacred Scriptures spoke of a Messiah who was to come and bring deliverance, not be crucified as a rebel. Their Messiah would be a conqueror, not a victim. And then to top it off, he was raised from the dead?

Suddenly, a third man joined these two on the road. He asked them what they were discussing. You would think that they saw a camel walking on its hind legs. Cleopas asked, "Are you the only visitor in Jerusalem who doesn't know the things that happened there in these days?" They were dumfounded that anyone could have missed the death of their Lord. Little did they know, they were speaking with the risen Lord himself.

Jesus initially responded with a rebuke, saying that their dissonant hearts were hesitant to believe all that the prophets had spoken. He pointed at Scripture, which at that time was only the OT. He asked them, "Wasn't it necessary for the Messiah to suffer these things and enter into his glory?" In other words, "The Scriptures spoke of me. How could you miss that?" Notice here that Jesus made a connection between their lack of faith and their misunderstanding of the OT. The reason they couldn't put the current events together theologically was because their view of the OT was out of whack. He did not tell them to wait for another Testament to be written—he indicated that the OT was enough for them to know the truth about him.

Jesus began to talk with them about how the Law, the prophets, and everything in between spoke of him. Then as they approached Emmaus, they invited Jesus to enjoy a meal together. But instead of staying the evening, he simply broke bread with them and departed supernaturally from their presence.

Afterwards, these disciples were no longer bickering about how their present understanding could be reconciled with their Messianic hopes. Instead, they were now confessing that their "hearts burned" as they heard Jesus explain the Scriptures to them. Their faith had been ignited because their eyes were opened to see how the OT spoke of everything that had happened, including Jesus's death and resurrection.

FANNING THE FLAME

This is a wonderful testimony indeed. So much so, we believe it is a worthy endeavor to fan this same flame of love for God and his Word today. That's why we wrote this book. We want to give you a glimpse of the OT's richness by seeing how Jesus Christ serves as its proper lens. We want to show that the New Testament (NT) consistently points to Jesus as the central interpretive key to understanding how the hopes of the OT were and will be fulfilled.

This is why this book is entitled *They Spoke of Me*. Jesus showed those disciples how various parts of the OT were written about himself. He revealed *how he was the key to unlocking the complete meaning of the OT* as God's Word. Therefore, what we want to do is cover nine examples (of many!) that illustrate Jesus's claim. Each individual chapter reveals how these subjects either foreshadow or describe assorted features about who Jesus is and/or what he has done. The focus here is not strictly on typology of Christ, nor is it meant to be exhaustive. Instead, we want to provide in a narrative format a few biblical portraits that will help readers see the centrality of Christ in all of Scripture.

We wrote this book together, with a common passion for God's Word to come alive for you. Though we both edited and contributed to portions of each chapter of the book, each author was assigned particular chapters to focus on. Brandon wrote the bulk of chapters 1, 2, 4, and 9, as well as the introductory and concluding chapters and recommended reading; Everett wrote the bulk of chapters 3, 5, 6, 7, and 8.

The first chapter examines how Jesus established a new humanity by acting as a new Adam, who recaptures all of the kingly dignity as God's image-bearer that the original Adam initially lost in the Fall. Chapter 2 transitions to a treatment of how Noah's story functions as an account about judgment and restoration, which only results in failure. Yet Jesus serves as a means of rescue from judgment that brings new creation instead. From there, the third chapter analyzes the way in which the mysterious man known as Melchizedek acted as a prelude to the role of a priestly king that Jesus would be for his people.

The fourth chapter moves beyond the book of Genesis to show how Jesus acts as a new Moses, fulfilling the expectations of the original lawgiver by mediating a new covenant. Chapter 5 shows that Jesus is not only prefigured in people's lives or certain books of the Bible; he is also a representation of God's covenant people Israel as a whole. This chapter will discuss how the story of Israel is retold and culminates in Jesus's life, death, and resurrection.

The sixth chapter discusses how Jesus serves as the premiere Davidic king who meets all the demands that the Law expected of Israel's true ruler. We will see that Jesus is not only a king like David, but the King of Kings himself. Chapter 7 highlights the way in which Jesus serves as the ultimate Temple wherein God's presence dwells in the midst his people in human form as opposed to a building made of stone.

Chapter 8 reveals how the Psalms have a dual focus. On the one hand, the Psalms were written to serve as Israel's hymnbook that could help Israel worship the Lord in every phase of its life as a nation. On the other hand, the Psalms also act as a treasure chest of accounts that are personified throughout the life and ministry of Jesus. This chapter will work through some key examples to illustrate this personification. And finally, the last chapter focuses on how the story of the prophet Jonah actually functions as a backdrop for some key moments in the life of Christ, particularly focusing on the dual accounts of boats in the middle of a storm and their three days in the belly of the whale and the grave.

We acknowledge at the outset that this book cannot match the wonderful experience that those two disciples had as they listened to the Teacher of Teachers riff on the OT. No doubt, it would have been great to eavesdrop on that conversation. But we pray that this book will help you see the beauty that might've resulted, and we hope it rekindles in you a passion for carefully reading all of God's Word, seeing Jesus emerge off its pages. Only then would we consider this book a success.

We pray that it will help you think through how to read, study, and teach the full story of the Bible. This book can be read cover-to-cover, or each chapter can be read on its own. Either way, we pray you quickly move from the pages of this book to the pages of Scripture itself.

1
HUMANITY

Oriole Park at Camden Yards, the current home of Major League Baseball's Baltimore Orioles, is one of the most iconic stadiums in America. One of its unique features is a bronze statue of Baltimore native and baseball great, Babe Ruth. Ruth was raised in Baltimore and experienced a particularly harsh upbringing, so the statue is named "Babe's Dream" because the artist wanted to portray Ruth's dream of one day escaping his childhood and playing in the big leagues. There he stands, gazing off into the future, cleats on his feet and a bat in his hand, dreaming of the day when he could escape the shackles of his life.

It is a beautiful piece of art. But the sculpture is merely an image of Ruth, an inexact representation of who and what he really was. Similarly, there is a sense of solidarity between mankind and "Babe's Dream." While the statue was made in someone's image, it's not an ultimate copy of the man it portrays. It is a shadow, a likeness. Likewise, we are made in the image of God, yet we are far removed from actually being just like him. Why is that?

THE IMAGE OF GOD AND THE KEYS OF CREATION

When we read the first two chapters of Genesis, we see that while God created all things, particular emphasis is placed on the creation of mankind. There is no mention of God creating angels, no discourse on other planets and galaxies, no detailed explanation of gravitational forces or the intricacies of the water cycle, and no extensive list of species of animals. Instead, Genesis 1 claims that the Lord brought into existence everything in creation. What was once chaotic and dark was now organized and life-giving. The narrative then quickly culminates in the creation of human beings, with Genesis 2 being dedicated entirely to the uniqueness of mankind.

We quickly discover humans share some similarities with animals in that they all need air and food to survive, but the parallels abruptly end after that. We see that Adam and Eve are described as being created in God's "image and likeness" (Gen. 1:26-27), an identity that no other creature can claim. These terms at least refer to the fact that they held a position of authority over creation, thereby being "like God" as his delegated rulers over the earth (cf., Gen. 1:28; 2:19-20).[1] Such a privilege meant that rather than merely coexisting with the rest of creation, God gave Adam and Eve the keys to it. They were given unique authority and dominion over all God had brought into being (Gen. 1:26).

Likewise, they were also ordered to "be fruitful and multiply and fill the earth and subdue it" (Gen. 1:28). The idea here is not merely that mankind would have children and propagate the species. More than that, they were to multiply humans who could then do the same, resulting in the spreading of God's image across the whole earth. Like ancient kings who later identified their kingdoms by placing their replica on key items (e.g., temples, coins, statues) to mark their territories, the Lord wanted to mark the earth with his created image-bearers. God did not place Adam and Eve in the Garden of Eden simply to tend to the garden—he wanted their offspring to eventually reign over the entire globe. The Garden was a starting point, not a final destination. Thomas Schreiner helpfully summarizes this idea: "God is the sovereign creator who extends his kingship over the world. But he extends his rule through human beings, for as God's image-bearers they must govern the world for God's glory and honor."[2]

We should also notice that at this time, Adam and Eve began in a state of innocence, having a right standing before God and each other. They reflected the very character and holiness of God, which meant that they began to reign over his creation "on earth as it is in heaven," a prayer of Jesus that we will return to shortly. But combined with these privileges, they were also expected to relate to the Lord within the parameters of certain stipulations. Along with the charge to be fruitful in reproduction, they were instructed to care for the earth in which they were placed (Gen. 2:15). And they were given a prohibition forbidding them from eating of one tree in the garden that Genesis calls "the tree of the knowledge of good and evil" (Gen. 2:16-17a).[3] If they were to eat of that tree, they would ultimately die (Gen. 2:17b).[4] Unfortunately, as we will see, Adam and Eve would not heed the Lord's warning and tragically fracture the goodness of Genesis 1 and 2.

THE FALL OF THE DIVINE IMAGE-BEARERS

Adam and Eve jeopardized their position as stewards over the earth when they considered being the Lord's equal as preferable to being his royal ambassadors. This notion first arose in the mind of Eve when a serpent, who is later identified as Satan himself (cf., Gen. 3:1a, 15; Rom. 16:20; Rev. 12:9, 20:2), tempted her by questioning the Lord's motives for excluding access to one tree, and even casting doubt upon whether his warnings about impending death were true (Gen. 3:1b, 4-5). The account begins with Eve standing before the serpent in the Garden. Eve was posed with a question-- "Did God really say, 'You shall not eat of any tree in the garden?'" -- to which Eve replied, "God said, 'You shall not eat of the fruit of the tree that is in the midst of the garden, neither shall you touch it, lest you die'" (Gen. 3:1-3). The serpent proceeded to do what he does best—twist the words of God just enough to make a lie sound like the truth. He told her, simply, that God did not want her to be like him. It was a blatant lie. But she ate.

Upon succumbing to this deception, Eve gave some of the fruit to Adam and he chose to eat as well. From here, this act of defiance immediately plunged creation into a cycle of spiritual chaos, robbing Adam and Eve of their dignity as God's delegated rulers. It even corrupted every facet of their everyday experiences, as we can see in their behavior after they ate from the tree. They made fig leaves to cover their nakedness because they became aware of their exposed vulnerability to one another (Gen. 3:7). Then as the Lord approached them, they hid in the garden only to be found and confronted (Gen. 3:8). After being forced to admit their guilt, the Lord announced certain curses that were to come upon them because of their sin. Perfect communion turned into hiding and finger-pointing from Adam and Eve, and judgment from God.

First, God stated that Eve's relationship to Adam would be gripped by conflict and her role in child-bearing would now be marked by painful suffering (Gen. 3:16). Further, he told Adam that his task in caring for the earth would be cursed because the land would now be wild and rugged; no longer would tending to the Garden be fully joyous. Instead of having authority over the earth, Adam would in fact return to the dust from which he came when he died (Gen. 3:17-19). Their sin created distressing obstacles that would work against the very things they were originally commissioned to do.

Essentially, then, Adam and Eve traded their dignity and freedom for the unrelenting bondage found in disobedience. They had quickly forgotten the declarations God had made, desiring to "make man in our image, according to our likeness" and granted them the joy of being able to "be fruitful, multiply, fill the earth, and subdue it" (Gen. 1:27-28). If they had remembered and believed their God-given purpose, Eve's response to Satan would have been clear: "I am already more like God than anything in creation. I have everything in my hands. What you're offering me is actually less than what I already have." So, ironically, in trying to be more like God, our first parents actually marred their God-likeness.[5] They introduced sin to humanity. They gave away their kingship and pure humanity. They lost their righteous standing before their Creator.

In Adam and Eve's singular act, the image of God was defaced and now we live with that reality today (Rom. 5:12). Satan disguised himself as a creature under the rule of mankind—a serpent—and overthrew his masters by convincing them that they needed more than what God had given them. They lost it all. Even after receiving curses of judgment, Adam and Eve were further banished from Eden. They were exiled, in a sense, from the place where they were first assigned to exercise their earthly dominion (Gen. 3:22-24). They were kicked out, forbidden from returning. As Desmond Alexander notes:

> [Because of Adam and Eve's] rebellious behavior, God's authority structures are overturned. The divine ordering of creation is rejected by the human couple, with disastrous consequences for all involved. Harmony gives way to chaos. As the early chapters of Genesis go on to reveal, people exercise dominion in the cruelest of ways.[6]

The once beautiful story of humanity became one of death, immorality, distrust, war, oppression, and idolatry. The first humans were God's appointed rulers of this world. God gave them the keys to creation and they did the unspeakable: they handed them over to Satan. Yet moving forward, we see that Scripture is not silent about how this transfer would be reversed. Through the seed of a woman (Gen. 3:15), a perfect man, Jesus Christ, would come in the very image of God and heal the brokenness of humanity. He would be the Messiah King who would one day rule over the earth with his people so that the failure of Adam and Eve could be rectified (e.g., Jer. 23:5; Zech. 9:9-13).

THE PERFECT IMAGE DETHRONES THE DECEIVER

Matthew 4, in an eerily similar scene to that of Genesis 3, tells of a man approached by Satan. Satan pulls out his top hat and begins to pull rabbits from within. "Turn these stones to bread, Son of God. Throw yourself from this temple and let God's angels catch you, Son of God. I will give you all the kingdoms of the world, Son of God." In response to these tactics, Jesus Christ, as the God-man, rejects Satan's offers with resilient steadfastness. He answers the way Eve should have: "God said to trust what he says. He has given me authority over creation. I have all I need in him. Now go away." Satan, being the serpent that he still is, slithers away in defeat.

What makes this confrontation so interesting is that the stage had been set previously in Matthew 3. This section ends with Jesus being baptized in one of the clearest depictions of the Trinity's unity. In the river, the Father calls him his Son, and the Holy Spirit comes down upon him. He then steps out of the river to begin a full-fledged assault on sin and death, and immediately heads to the wilderness to defeat Satan. The first verse of Matthew 4 says "*then* Jesus was led by the Spirit into the wilderness *to be* tempted." This is crucial: Jesus was not caught off guard by the devil's appearance. Satan did not trap Jesus—Jesus trapped Satan. Jesus came out of the water and went into the wilderness for a purpose.

We see in this story that God the Son, the very image of God (Col. 1:15), stepped into human history as a man to restore the image and likeness of God in man. In the wilderness, he showed that the keys to creation did not belong to the Enemy who had tried to steal them so long ago. Man was inserted back into his rightful place through the God-man. Here Alexander is helpful in reminding us that in the Gospel of John in particular, "Jesus himself refers to Satan as the 'ruler [or 'prince'] of this world' (Jn. 12:31; 14:30; 16:11). Each time Jesus declares that he has come in order to overthrow him."[7] And that's exactly what he did. Instead of being deceived by Satan, he withstood and defeated him.

BRINGING HEAVEN TO THE EARTH

As we saw in the beginning of creation, all that God had made was declared good. His will was being done perfectly on the earth. However, after that destructive bite of fruit, this was no longer the case. This is why Jesus arrived on the scene—to remedy that, to harmonize heaven's will with the created order. And the first step was to dethrone Satan so a new man could be re-throned.

Following Jesus's baptism and temptations in the wilderness, Matthew 5-7 shows Jesus teaching on the kingdom of God (or heaven), the place where his Father's will is still perfectly done. This sermon is his first recorded treatise on living according to his Father's kingdom, which is the way it would have been on earth without the Eden incident. Throughout the message, Jesus not only embodied his teachings personally; he taught it to others and instructed his disciples to pray for God's kingdom to come to the earth.

1. Jesus's Prayers for Heaven to Come to Earth

In Matthew 6:9-10, Jesus taught his disciples to pray, beginning with, "Our Father in heaven, your name be honored as holy. *Your kingdom come. Your will be done on earth as it is in heaven.*" It is easy to overlook the implications of this prayer, namely because it is recited almost solemnly in churches and homes around the world. But think about this—the earth actually was once *as it is in heaven*. God dwelled with man here, on this earth, in the Garden of Eden. But that peaceful state was turned upside down by sin.

As we recall, though, Jesus came to repair what was broken. God stepped into human history. He declared that creation was being taken back from Satan in the wilderness—and sin and death were next. So here he is telling his disciples to pray for the world to be like Eden again, or more emphatically, better than Eden ever was. This was not a wishful prayer for sojourners in a lost world (though it is partially that); this was a prayer of expectation and action. Jesus did not tell them to pray for something that would not be answered.

In addition to this prayer, Jesus emphasized this heaven-on-earth process by continuing to teach about the kingdom through parables and performing supernatural acts that today are often called miracles. Parables explained the cost and ethics of the kingdom of God, while his miracles expressed its power over everything related to the present age of sin including Satan, demons, sickness, and death. Jesus's ministry, then, was a glimpse or preview of what heaven on earth would look like.

2. Jesus's Teachings about How Heaven Can Come to Earth

Jesus's parables are stories about the nature of God's kingdom. They are small windows into heaven's perspective. More than that, they are also challenges to respond appropriately to God's way of doing things. One prime example of this dynamic can be seen in one of his earliest parables in the Gospels, dubbed "The Parable of the Sower." Here a sower goes out to plant seeds. Some of the seeds fall along the wayside and are devoured by birds. Some fall on rocky ground, and though the plant sprang up quickly, it had no roots and died out. Some fell on thorny ground, and though they sprang up, the thorns choked them out before they could produce fruit. Finally, some fell on good soil and not only sprang up, but yielded much fruit.

After telling this parable, Jesus was asked why he spoke in parables in the first place. He simply answered that the kingdom of God was a mystery everyone would not receive. He then explained the parable and clarified the meaning of his story. The seed represents the word (or the message) of God. The seed fell all over the place and many heard it, but only the ones with a certain kind of heart, or receptive soil, would allow the word to plant roots in their hearts and bear fruit (Lk. 8:11-15). And the fruit that derives from good soil is indicative of a person who is a citizen of God's kingdom. The reason being that only heaven can bear such fruit. Unlike Adam and Eve who brought about thorns and thistles, the kingdom of God reaps heavenly fruit in the hearts of those who believe.

3. Jesus Exercising Heavenly Acts on Earth

While parables tell us things about the kingdom, Jesus's miracles display its power. When he healed the blind, told the crippled to get up and walk, or raised people from the dead, he was giving glimpses of life in the kingdom of God by showing its sheer command and authority over the effects of sin on creation. They showed that physical infirmities like blindness, lameness, and ultimately death were not the way the world should be. Though they were introduced into the world because of Adam and Eve's sin, Jesus was showing that creation had not been abandoned. It was going to be renewed once again.

In addition, the power exhibited through miracles flowed out of Jesus's divine, heaven-sent authority over creation. Adam and Eve were expelled from the Garden and left helpless apart from the grace of God. Still, Jesus came to their defense, defeating Satan and as the God-man and King of Kings, ultimately restoring heaven and earth in a redeemed state that transcends even what Adam had before he fell.

Finally, the miracles performed by Jesus the man revealed the way in which the earth would be renewed after disobedience of the first man. When earth came under the jurisdiction of sin and death, enmity was created between God and man. But as the God-man, Jesus gave a snapshot of heaven for the earth to see. In his excellent primer on Jesus's miracles, Jared Wilson observes, "Jesus's miracles are the very windows into heaven, and through them heaven is spilling into earth like sunlight through panes whose shades have been violently rolled up."[8]

REVEALING HEAVEN THROUGH HUMANITY

Jesus's preaching and miracle-working are essential to our understanding of his heaven-brought, renewed kind of humanity. But we must point out that Jesus was not simply a different kind of man. Christ was not a mere replica of Adam before he fell. No, he was the eternal Son of God who was sent from heaven to become incarnate in the person of Jesus.[9] So as the God-man, he is fully man *and* fully God. As the apostle John reminds us in the prologue of his Gospel:

> *In the beginning was the Word, and the Word was with God, and the Word was God. He was with God in the beginning. All things*

> *were created through him, and apart from him not one thing was created that has been created . . . The Word became flesh and dwelt among us. We observed his glory, the glory as the one and only Son from the Father, full of grace and truth.* (Jn. 1:1-3, 14)

Here is the point: Christ's divinity is essential to understanding how he defines what it truly means to be human. Both his deity and humanity show how heaven's creator and earth's original ruler can come together in one person to remedy the divorce between heaven and creation. Only God can live perfectly and forgive sins; only a man can shed real blood and die a real death.

1. Divine Authority over Sin for Humanity

A superb example of this dynamic can be seen in a miracle recorded in Matthew 9:1-8. Jesus encountered a paralyzed man, and he told him two things. He said "your sins are forgiven" and "get up and walk." The first statement got him in trouble with the scribes. They accused him of blasphemy for claiming that he could forgive the man's sins—after all, only God could do that! Jesus answered their charge not with an apology or a clarification, but with an affirmation. He explained that he had authority to forgive sins, and then doubled-down by telling the man to walk home.

While the scribes were probably not happy, the on-lookers "were afraid, and they glorified God, who had given such authority to men." The crowd just saw a man exercise divine authority over the spiritual and physical calamity of the paralytic man. While they surely did not have a full concept of the Trinity at this point, they witnessed something that they had clearly never witnessed before. Magicians and wonder-workers were not entirely uncommon in that time, yet a man claiming to forgive sins was rare indeed.

2. Divine Victory over Death for Humanity

Coupled with the point above, God's mission to defeat death also had to be completed through a human for several reasons. One is that the Old Testament and New Testament both confirm that the shedding of blood is required for the atonement of sins (Ex. 29:10-14; Lev. 17:11; Heb. 9:22). But there is an immediate problem here. God is immaterial spirit. He is not made of flesh and bone. So, somehow he had to become a man so he could bleed and die. Among the persons of the triune God, the Father sent his Son to become a man so he could hang on the cross, become a curse for sinners, and shed sacrificial blood for the sins of mankind (Matt. 26:28; Jn. 1:36; Gal. 3:13; Eph. 1:7; 1 Jn. 2:2). Second, the Son became a man in order to live a sinless life and qualify to be a worthy sacrifice (Jn. 19:4; 2 Cor. 5:21; Heb. 4:15; 1 Jn. 3:5). An atoning sacrifice, especially for a new covenant, had to be without blemish. And third, Christ became a man not only so he could die; he became a man to defeat death through resurrection (Acts 2:24; Rom. 6:4-11; 2 Tim. 1:10; Heb. 2:14; Rev. 1:18).

To put it plainly, Christ became an actual man to reverse the mistakes of the first one. He was the means whereby God would keep his original promise to restore mankind to himself (Gen. 3:15, 17:6-8; 2 Sam. 7:12-14; Jer. 31:33; Ezek. 36:22-28). Furthermore, Scripture is clear that Jesus did not come as some ethereal, nebulous spirit, representing some ideal of God's love. The Son of God assumed human flesh to enact God's love with his bare hands. Thus, Jesus's genuine humanity in genuine history was a living, breathing example of God's genuine faithfulness.[10]

3. Divine Triumph for Heaven

Another factor to keep in mind is that while Christ became a man so he could bring heaven to earth, he also reconciled earth to heaven. We see this dynamic in the NT descriptions of Christ's ascension. Here, following his resurrection, he appeared to various disciples for some forty days (Acts 1:3). Afterwards, he then ascended to heaven to be "seated at the right hand of the Father" (Lk. 24:51; Acts 2:33). Now that same man, "who tasted death for everyone," intercedes for mankind in heaven, "crowned with glory and honor" (Heb. 2:9). Consequently, no one can condemn those who are in Jesus because he did not cease to be their Savior once he left earth (Rom. 8:34; Heb. 7:25). Instead, we discover that this journey back to heaven's domain was the culmination of his victory over death, man's greatest foe. The cross, the empty tomb, and the ascension are the exclamation points that emphasize Christ's success in representing heaven's kingdom as a man.

JESUS AS THE NEW ADAM

As we have seen, God the Son took it upon himself to be the human that Adam and Eve were supposed to be. He came to make the Lord's Prayer true. He came to undo and redo all that the first humans did. He came to fulfill the promises of God by becoming true humanity. Jesus restores what humanity destroyed. This is why the NT focuses so much on the theme of how heaven will be reconciled to a healed earth by someone who represents both domains.

1. Jesus Is a Second Adam

One of the most well-known depictions of Jesus in this way comes from the apostle Paul, who describes him as a new substitute for the first Adam. The idea that Paul makes here coincides well with the content of Matthew 3-7, Christ's parables and miracles, his death and resurrection, the ascension, and the promise of new creation (which is alluded to Rev. 21-22 quite strikingly). More specifically, this motif is clearly emphasized in two particular passages by Paul: Romans 5:12-19 and 1 Corinthians 15:20-22, 42-49.

When we read these passages, we notice numerous contrasts that Paul makes between Adam and Christ. For example, Adam came from the earth while Jesus came from heaven (1 Cor. 15:46-47). Adam disobeyed God, but Jesus obeyed the Father (Rom. 5:19). Adam forfeited the grace of God and caused sin to abound, but Jesus restored the grace of God, causing it to abound (Rom. 5:15, 20). Adam stayed in the grave while Jesus walked out of it (1 Cor. 15:20-22). Condemnation and death came through Adam, but forgiveness and life came through Jesus (Rom. 5:17-18).

The key to see in these comparisons is not merely the predicament that the first Adam created for humanity. Rather, the bigger point is that Christ is both the face of God and humanity. Heaven met earth the day Mary gave birth to a baby boy in Bethlehem. This is why we do not build idols to see God—we look at Jesus, the image of God (Col. 1:15). We don't look at Adam as the ultimate excuse for our sin—we look at Jesus, the ultimate destroyer of our sin (1 Cor. 15:57). God and man are reconciled through Jesus Christ, and one day the God-man will step into human history again to finally restore this divide (Rev. 19-22).

2. Jesus Is a New Humanity

Not only does Jesus overcome the barriers that divide heaven from earth—he also tears down the walls that divide the peoples of the earth. We see a need for this all throughout Scripture. For instance, before Adam and Eve are cast out of the Garden, they were immediately at odds with each other as seen in their attempts to cover themselves, and in Adam's later attempt to blame Eve for his disobedience (Gen. 3:12). This divisiveness is further intensified when one of their sons, Cain, actually becomes so enraged against his brother Abel that he murders him (Gen. 4:8). This kind of divisiveness between people continues in various ways in the OT history and by the time of Christ, the supreme expression of it was between Jews and Gentiles.

The Jews were God's covenant people as opposed to all the other surrounding nations. And on top of this theological heritage that Israel possessed, there was a larger reason for animosity because the Romans ruled over the holy land at that time. In a sense, Israel was experiencing the worst kind of exile: living in their homeland but not having control of it. God's people being strangers in other lands is a glaring picture of humanity being at odds with itself and the creation around it.

Eventually as the new covenant community, the Church began to grow and expand. Of primary note, Gentiles were now becoming recipients of the blessings of salvation along with believing Jews. Recognizing the significance of this, Paul mentions in his letter to the Ephesians that Gentiles were originally on the outside looking in when it came to God's covenant promises (Eph. 2:11-12). However, in Christ, both believing Jews and Gentiles were reconciled to each other as well as God. Jesus was Israel's Messiah, but even more than that, he was humanity's Messiah.[11] So just as Jesus brought peace between sinners and God, he also has established peace between sinners of different backgrounds. Thus, Jesus is not only a new Adam who heals the earth. He also restores solidarity between people.

3. Jesus Brings a New City

A final example of how Jesus unites heaven and earth can be seen in the last book of the Bible, describing the definitive result of Jesus's restoration of creation at his final return. Revelation 21 illustrates a stunning scene in which heaven and earth are united, "a graphic representation that God's kingdom *has* come and his will *is* forevermore to be accomplished on this earth—just as it has always been in heaven."[12] We then witness a beautiful and familiar scene:

> *Then he showed me the river of the water of life, clear as crystal, flowing from the throne of God and of the Lamb down the middle of the city's main street.* The tree of life was on each side of the river, *bearing twelve kinds of fruit, producing its fruit every month. The leaves of the tree are for healing the nations, and there will no longer be any curse. The throne of God and of the Lamb will be in the city, and his servants will worship him.*

They will see his face, and his name will be on their foreheads. Night will be no more; people will not need the light of a lamp or the light of the sun, because the Lord God will give them light, and they will reign forever and ever. (Rev. 22:1-5)

The tree from which Adam and Eve ate gets a lot of publicity, and rightly so. The fruit of that tree dramatically altered the course of human history. But when our first parents were kicked out of Eden, they were separated from another tree: the tree of life (Gen. 2:9). So expulsion from the Garden meant an introduction to death. Access to the tree of life was no more.

However, as we see above in Revelation 22, the tree of life is once again accessible through the work of Jesus. Sin and death are eradicated, the nations are healed, and his servants are once again reigning with him on the earth. This vision fits perfectly with Jesus's command that we pray for God's kingdom to come to earth. Why? Because his disciples are to live in the expectation of that world to come.

GOD LIVING IN MAN

In C. S. Lewis's *Perelandra*, the main character, Ransom, travels to Venus and intervenes in the antagonist's plot to introduce evil to the King and Queen of the planet, initiating Earth-like chaos on Venus. Ransom prevents the King and Queen from falling into temptation and destroying peace on the planet. The King and Queen are given divine dominion over Venus and celebrate the beginning of a utopian society. Ransom then returns to Earth to continue to fight evil there.

The biblical and theological parallels in *Perelandra* are remarkable. It is a glimpse into what the world might have been like if Adam and Eve had not fallen. The King and Queen of Venus are the anti-Adam and Eve; our King and Queen actually did introduce evil into the world. Yet the King of Kings did not merely intervene—he *became* the King by living a life perfectly as a man and *became* the Ransom so that a redeemed humanity could once again reign with him.

Likewise, when Jesus ascended back to heaven, he sent us the Holy Spirit that we might be renewed into the image of God (Eph. 4:24; Col. 3:10). Not only that, Jesus even told his disciples that through the Holy Spirit, they would do even greater works than he did (Jn. 14:12-17). And on top of that, we join in God's plan of redemption through the way in which we worship him with our lives. As Kevin Vanhoozer has said, "Disciples imitate the Son ... when they too glorify God in their bodies by performing works of grateful obedience."[13]

This all appears astounding on the surface—and it is. But Jesus is merely reminding us that he came to destroy darkness and that we are to take the gospel, the good news of redemption, to the world by his authority. Also as Jesus's emissary within believers, the Spirit empowers us to take the gospel to the ends of earth, pointing to the day when the King of Kings will reign over the completely restored creation, where the effects of Adam and Eve's blunder will be mere memories.

In the meantime, like "Babe's Dream," we are but image-bearers of the Image. And we look off into the distance, awaiting the day when we can fully escape the shackles of this life. Yet unlike the sculpture, we are not lifeless and stationary. We are image-bearers of God on a mission to reflect the power of Christ as we await his return to bring heaven to earth.

DISCUSSION

List a few truths you learned in this chapter that you'd not seen in Scripture before.

How do these truths apply to your life?

Why are these truths important to share with others?

2
NOAH

Receiving the love of a parent is one of the most common and needed human experiences. But sometimes instead of warm hugs and kisses, children might get a little big for their britches and require discipline. Whether it's for sassing their parents, outright defiance, or being caught in a lie or wrongdoing, a good parent knows that bad behavior must be corrected.

However, there are other times, as children grow older into adulthood, where potential streaks of rebellion can reach a point when more severe action is required. Such instances occur as people transition from adolescent mischievousness to outright and willful sin. When this happens, God sometimes transforms a person's heart in ways that no one else can. It's difficult to put an adult in timeout, after all. So God often uses life circumstances to help enable people to come to their senses spiritually. In many occasions, this scenario plays itself out when prodigals come home to experience the beauty of reconciliation.

Other times, though, people refuse to repent. This can be tragic, especially if the rebellion is life-long and there appears to be no expectation of change. But when someone chooses to live a life of obedience, when they come to their spiritual senses, these stories provide glimmers of hope.

Both of these circumstances—blessing to those who live obediently and judgment to those who live defiantly—come up constantly throughout the story of the Bible. As we will see and have already seen, the Bible is full of stories about rebellion and reconciliation, judgment and grace. One place where they are echoed quite loudly is in the story of Noah.

THE STORY OF NOAH

The famous (or infamous, depending on who you ask) story of Noah and the flood fills Sunday school classes, kids' books, and Christian art. The depictions are always the same—a bunch of cute zoo animals on a boat captained by a jolly old man who looks like a prehistoric Santa Claus, with the sun shining overhead and clouds puffier than an extra-large cotton candy at the fair. If you had no backstory, you might think that Noah loaded up some exotic animals and decided to tour the Atlantic Ocean.

In other contexts, you might think the flood was an ancient recounting of an angry God who arbitrarily hates people. Non-Christians are especially susceptible to this idea, though even many Christians also assume that "the God of the Old Testament" is like a petulant child with a magnifying glass, scorching us like ants out of sheer maniacal pleasure.

The flood narrative, then, is often misconstrued in ways that cause people to misunderstand the Bible's larger story. The truth is, both of these polarized postures are wrong. The flood is actually a sign of both judgment *and* grace. Likewise, it is not an isolated story in the Old Testament; rather, it is one piece of an unfolding story told from Genesis to Revelation. Let's take a further look.

1. Noah's Purpose

Noah's role on the biblical stage can be broken down into four parts.[14] The first segment comes when we are introduced to him through a prediction that is made by his father Lamech (Gen. 5:29). Lamech prophesied that Noah would bring much needed comfort to the human race in light of the fact that the earth (or "land") had been cursed after Adam's sin. So, as a means of renewing the earth, God would use Noah. Somehow the world would be relieved, even if for a moment, from the onslaught of evil that had come upon it. Noah would serve as a kind of intermediary who would bring comfort to humanity, a reprieve from the heavy burden that Adam's sin had brought upon the everyday responsibilities of labor (Gen. 3:17-19).

The gist of this prophecy is later alluded to in Genesis 9:20 after the great flood, when Noah is said to begin repopulating the earth through the initial growth of the families produced by his three sons, Shem, Ham, and Japheth. Also, Noah is said to have started farming once more and even planted a vineyard (Gen. 9:20).[15] Granted, as we shall see, this act led to problematic behavior. But still, Noah's life led to a new start for creation wherein the upsurge of evil was judged—and humanity was given another chance.

2. Noah and the Flood

The second major scene in Noah's life that Scripture discusses is the most well-known—the great flood. We read that when the Lord decided to take this measure, it was no trivial matter. God was not throwing a hissy-fit or reacting hastily. Rather, we read that his decision came out a deep grief for what sin had done to the world that he had originally created as "good." Genesis 6:5-8 tells us:

> *When the Lord saw that human wickedness was widespread on the earth and that every inclination of the human mind was nothing but evil all the time, the Lord regretted that he had made man on the earth, and he was deeply grieved. Then the Lord said, "I will wipe mankind, whom I created, off the face of the earth, together with the animals, creatures that crawl, and birds of the sky – for I regret that I made them." Noah, however, found favor with the Lord.*

There is such tragic commentary here. Wickedness had filled the earth to the point that God regretted even making mankind. This is not to say that God did not foresee sin coming into the world, nor is it to say that he ran out of options. His "regret" is an outflow of his care for his creation. His grief is borne out of his love, holiness, and demand for justice, not out of confusion or disillusioned expectations. And the flood shows the extreme measures he will take to fight sin and redeem creation. In fact, the flood teaches us about some of the core characteristics of God, including his hatred of sin, his demand to judge those who commit sin, and his grace that is extended to anyone who repents and follows him in obedience.

So, as evil continued to flood the earth spiritually, the Lord determined that he would send a literal flood as a consequence. Scripture says that Noah was a righteous and blameless man, meaning that he knew God, communed with him, and strove to live his life in a way that honored him. The point was not that Noah had no sin; it's that Noah lived for the Lord in spite of his sin. In contrast to Noah's godliness and that of his family, the remaining masses continued in engage in wickedness so much so that Genesis says that the earth was filled with violence. The Lord looked upon the earth and saw that humanity had given itself over to corruption (Gen. 6:11-12).

God then instructs Noah on how to make preparations by constructing an ark so he, his family, and animals can survive. Noah follows the Lord's commands and builds the ark according to the Lord's specifications. As promised, when the impending flood did arrive, Noah and his family entered the ark so they could be spared. Water came from the heavens and from the depths below, creating a sandwich effect in which the earth was being engulfed by water from both sides. It rained for forty days and nights with the rising waters covering the highest mountains, killing every person, land-roaming animal, and bird. The waters prevailed over the earth for 150 days, and every living thing was "wiped off the earth" (Gen. 7:23-24).

This overwhelming act of judgment marked a tragic point in redemptive history. Though we shall see shortly that it was not the last word, the flood served as a monumental benchmark displaying the huge gap that had grown between God's holiness and man's sinfulness. Not only that, but it also acted as a picture of future judgments that the Lord would enact upon people because of their wickedness (cf., Isa. 24:18; Zeph. 1:2-18; Amos 5:8) and as we will see, parts of the NT teach that the flood actually prefigures the return of Christ to establish his kingdom on the earth.[16]

3. Noah and a Special Covenant

The third part of Noah's story entails his deliverance after the flood waters subsided. We read that the Lord "remembered" Noah in the ark, meaning that he was not going to go back on his promise to preserve Noah nor his earlier prediction that he would defeat the serpent through the seed of a woman. In time, the waters receded and the ark reached a new shoreland at last. Noah embarked off the ark with a thankful heart. He then offered an acceptable sacrifice to the Lord. And from here, God promises to "never again curse the ground because of human beings, even though the inclination of the human heart is evil from youth onward" (Gen. 8:21). So sin wasn't fully erased, but God's judgment was nonetheless sufficient for the time.

Finally, he declared a covenant agreement with Noah that would be a benefit to all his descendants. The Lord guaranteed that he would never destroy the earth again with a flood (Gen. 9:11). As a sign of this promise, God said that he would place his "bow" (rainbow) in the clouds as a reminder that humankind would never be wiped out by a divine deluge. The basic point was that even though man's sinfulness was great, God's grace would always be greater. This is a critical truth, one that is consistently emphasized in the Bible. When sin strikes a 5.0 on the spiritual Richter scale, grace hits a 6.0; sin hits a 6.0; and then grace reaches a 7.0. Grace is always greater, and the rainbow was to be a continual reminder of that fact.

4. Noah and a New Start

The fourth and final part of Noah's story comes on the heels of God's covenant with him. Here we are reminded of why God shows grace to people—because they are sinners. Perfect people don't need forgiveness. Up to this point, we have seen that while mankind had become almost unbearably wicked, God remained committed to his promise back in

Genesis 3 that he would send a redeemer. Wiping out every human on earth would be quite the drastic move if he wanted to redeem mankind. This is why he showed favor on one man—Noah. Through Noah and his family, God would start with a new first family, another Adam and Eve. Genesis 9:1-4 sounds quite familiar:

> God blessed Noah and his sons and said to them, "Be fruitful and multiply and fill the earth. The fear and terror of you will be in every living creature on the earth, every bird of the sky, every creature that crawls on the ground, and all the fish of the sea. They are placed under your authority. Every creature that lives and moves will be food for you; as I gave the green plants, I have given you everything. However, you must not eat meat with its lifeblood in it."

When we compare these comments with God's original commission to Adam and Eve in the first chapters of Genesis, we see similar ingredients—"be fruitful and multiply," every creature is under your authority," and "don't eat this one thing."

Here, we see God once again giving mankind grace, even when they didn't deserve it. He did not demote them to the level of animals, nor did he transfer his image to another creature. And, of course, he kept his promise to move history toward complete redemption. A flood was not going to be the end of the story—a crushed serpent's head and a redeemed humanity would be.

Now despite these clear parallels, we have already seen from the previous chapter that Noah could never be a new kind of Adam. As godly as he was, he still remained a natural descendant of the first one. Sin was still in his DNA. We are reminded of this in the last part of Noah's account, where we read that after planting a vineyard, he reaped a harvest and became drunk from wine he had made. From here, his sons found him in a shameful stupor. Two of his boys, Shem and Japheth treated him with honor by covering him with a garment because he was naked. But his third son, Ham, dishonored him somehow. After Noah later came to his senses, he realized what Ham had done and announced a curse on him as well as his descendants through his son Canaan. What we find then is that not long after Noah left the ark and embarked on a newly-washed earth, sin and curses arrived right back on the scene (Gen. 9:20-25).

Thus, we see something critical about ourselves in how Noah's story ends. On the one hand, God used Noah and his family to preserve Adam's descendants, despite their inclinations to be just like Adam. Noah stands as an example of someone who imperfectly obeyed the Lord because of faith in his promises (cf., Ezek. 14:14, 20; Heb. 11:7). Still, on the other hand, Noah is a sober reminder that God's judgment upon the sin of some does not eliminate the sin in others. While the ark saved Noah from the flood, it could never save him from his own sinfulness. A different kind of vessel would have to do that—a heavenly one personified in Jesus himself.

JESUS AS ANOTHER NOAH

So far, we have seen that the account of Noah's flood is not simply a Sunday school story about sunny skies and rainbows. Real people died, and real sin was punished in a real flood. At the same time, Noah's life is not merely a grim story about fury and death. Even though God did exercise judgment upon the masses because they refused to turn from their sins, he still showed grace to those who followed him. The problem, though, is that Noah's capacity to build an ark and survive the flood did not include any ability to escape the corruption within his own heart. There needed to be another telling of the Noah story that would not end in sin or curses—one that would conclude with consistent obedience, salvation, and a guarantee that no judgment in any form (water or otherwise) would ever be needed again.

Such a solution arrives on the scene, beginning with John the Baptist's announcement that the Messiah was on his way (Matt. 3). John served as a prophetic bridge between the hopes of old covenant Israel and their fulfillment in the upcoming ministry of Jesus. But Jesus's arrival did not only mean that the Lord's salvation would be provided; it also meant that divine judgment would come for all those who didn't repent. So just as Noah implored people to prepare for divine judgment that was to come upon the earth, John proclaimed that Christ would extend mercy to those who repent and enact retribution on those who do not. And it is here in this contrast that we find the NT occasionally making connections between Noah and Jesus. We will briefly mention four here.

1. Jesus's Return Will Reflect the Judgment of Noah's Flood

One crucial link is the fact that Jesus preached to a generation of people who, for the most part, imitated the very attitudes of Noah's generation. And even more amazingly, Jesus predicted that the kind of crowds that rejected God in Noah's day would also be around when he returned to establish his kingdom on the earth. We see this, for example, when Jesus spoke of his coming in judgment as the divine-human Son of Man. He claimed that he would come and vindicate his people, and when he did, he posed the question as to whether he would find any faith on the earth at that time (Lk. 18:8).The implied answer to his question is either a "no" altogether or "not much." Noah could relate.

An even more explicit parallel occurs in what is known today as the Olivet Discourse. Here, Jesus was sitting on the Mount of Olives just east of the city of Jerusalem. He had been asked some pointed questions about a recent prediction he had made about the future destruction of the Temple. In discussing these matters, he also mentions some features related to the Son of Man's return to judge humanity and redeem his people (cf., Matt. 24:36-40; Lk. 17:26-27).

He claimed here that no one knew the hour of his coming. It would be unexpected like a thief who invades a home or a master who arrives at a time in which his servants do not expect him. In fact, it would shock people just as the flood did in Noah's time. Jesus said that people in Noah's day were so consumed with their own lives and debauchery that they were oblivious to the watery annihilation that was coming–that is, until Noah and his family entered the ark. But by then it was too late. In the same way, Jesus said that when he returned, just as the flood took Noah's unbelieving generation away in judgment, so likewise would unbelievers at his return be suddenly taken away.

Therefore, the climate in which Noah lived would be replicated again in two ways when Jesus returns. First, people will ignore Jesus's pleas for their repentance, choosing instead to cast their desires on the trivial pleasures of life. And their willful ignorance will in no way delay or deter the worldwide judgment that will ensue them. Second, the rebellion of the unbelieving masses will incur the same result that occurred in Noah's day, except without any water being used. Instead of a flood washing away sinful humanity, Jesus will return to remove his enemies, defeat Satan, and allow his people to inherit a truly renewed and redeemed creation. When Jesus finally returns for good, there won't be any sinful seeds ready to sprout up again.

2. Jesus Brings Salvation like the Ark of Noah

A second major connection is the fact that Jesus delivers us from judgment like the ark did for Noah. The apostle Peter actually emphasizes this parallel in his first letter. In a passage that contains some extremely difficult comments to interpret, Peter says at one point that the Lord was patient with humanity during the time when Noah was building the ark (1 Pet. 3:19-22). Afterwards, this ancient boat served as the means of delivering Noah and his family. In the same way, Christians now experience a similar deliverance that previews the final judgment of Christ.

By way of illustration, Peter says that the flood is a kind of ancient simulation of what happens in Christian baptism. Originally, Noah and his family were saved by being plunged into water and brought up out of it because of the ark's protection. Now, believers are baptized in water because of a clear conscience before the Lord and the desire to be identified with Jesus, who was plunged into the earth and ultimately raised from the dead. So, in a sense, Jesus himself allows his followers to be saved from judgment and death, and our being plunged into the water and brought up out of it reflects that truth. Yet, whereas the wooden ark acted as an instrument of redemption for Noah's physical life, a Roman wooden cross served as the means for delivering us. Just as Noah obeyed God by climbing onto a boat to save a few, Jesus obeyed his Father by climbing onto a cross to save many.

3. Jesus Succeeds Where Noah (and Adam) Failed

A third way that Jesus intersects with the story of Noah is his establishment of a new creation. However, his redemption surpasses what Noah received after the flood and even what Adam experienced *before* he sinned. This factor is important for several reasons.

We have already dealt with many of the important details about Adam's life in the previous chapter. However, as we mentioned earlier, Genesis describes Noah's chance to begin again—mirroring the mandate given to Adam and Eve at the beginning of creation. But the unfortunate truth was that despite Noah's godliness and righteous standing before the Lord, he still possessed the fallen nature of his original ancestor Adam. So even with all of rebellious humanity out of the way and under the water, Noah and his family still repeated the same basic sinful tendencies.

The good news is that despite Noah's shortcomings, he was still linked to the initial promise that the Lord gave to Adam—that the seed of a woman would eventually defeat the serpent. We see this in the fact that Noah belonged to a special line that was traced from Adam through the line of Seth, which was a family line that obeyed God.[17] From here, Noah became the one who preserved humanity and ultimately served as a precursor for the sacred line of the OT patriarchs including Abraham, Isaac, and Jacob. And obviously from here, it would mean that Noah was part of the Messianic line because from the patriarchs came the tribes of Israel including Judah—the same clan from which Christ himself would come (cf., Matt. 1:1-17; Heb. 7:14; Rev. 5:5)

So, then, while Noah was another version of a fallen Adam, by God's grace he also served as a remnant line through which the serpent-crushing seed would come. Christ was not a kind of Noah 2.0; rather he was an

Adam 2.0, but an Adam who would not fall prey to the same moral pitfalls to which Adam and Noah succumbed. In a sense, even though Noah was like all of us in that he was a child of the old Adam, God graciously used him to prefigure a new Adam. Jesus Christ became the man Adam chose not to be and the man Noah never could be. Adam was born without sin but chose to sin; Noah was born into sin and could never escape it. But instead of temporarily obeying his Father only to succumb to failure, Jesus obeyed perfectly so he could be given the keys of death and Hades, thereby being authorized to judge sin and defeat Satan (Rev. 1:18).

4. Jesus Ensures the End of Judgment

Let's now look at our fourth and final parallel between Jesus and Noah. As we have seen, the flood teaches several things. First, it's a sober reminder that God judges sinners who do not repent. Also, it's a precursor to a final judgment that will affect all of humanity. Yet it is laced with promises of grace, because the flood was part of a bigger story that includes promises of restoration and salvation. Even in washing most of humanity away, God proved to be faithful because he spared one family that would lead to the birth of the Savior. History was being pushed toward a better day—a day when the earth would be restored. God is not rocketing us out of this world. No, like the flood story, he's going to keep us right here. But this time, we'll be in a new creation that will never taste sin or a curse again (Rev. 21-22). Creation will not groan in chaos or be at odds with humanity. It will be restored, and a new Adam will lead a redeemed humanity to rule over it.

These grand truths are tied together beautifully in the Book of Revelation. Though many readers become fascinated with all kinds of doomsday predictions when trying to understand this book, one major theme that emerges is how God actually views the victory that Jesus has over death, sin, and Satan himself. And sometimes amidst the visionary descriptions, portions of Noahic imagery emerge.

For instance, in Revelation 4:1-11, we are given a wonderful glimpse of a scene in a heavenly throne room. John, the author, draws upon imagery from prophets like Isaiah and Ezekiel, who had visionary encounters with the Lord, to describe what he sees. He also appeals to natural phenomenon that were originally used in the OT to describe occasions where the Lord appeared to Israel, such as the thunder storms on Mount Sinai and the shiny, glowing ground that Moses and Israel's elders encountered when they were with the Lord. John says that he saw a throne and from behind it came all kinds of sounds of lightening and blasting peals of thunder. There were lamps burning around the throne and before it was a kind of crystal or glass sea. At the center were all kinds of heavenly creatures who worshipped the Lord. And among all these fascinating features, John also mentions that something like rainbow, something like an emerald, that glistened with color. The brilliant covenantal colors that God set in the earthly sky were actually indicative of his presence in heaven. After exercising his authority to judge the earth by sending the flood, he chose to display that authority in a gracious way by placing a visible bow in the physical heavens.

Such language happens again in 10:1, where we are told that John saw an angelic being come down out of heaven with cosmic majesty being clothed with a cloud, his face shining like the sun, and a rainbow being on his head. Again, the idea being that this angel, whoever he may be,[18] exercised heavenly authority because he was granted a royalty-like appearance including a colorful bow of majesty. So, we see this imagery of a bow or rainbow in the sky, reflecting God's glory.

Finally, the Noahic promise that was symbolized by the physical manifestation of a rainbow in the sky comes to completion at the end of Revelation. We read that after Jesus returns to judge the nations with his mouth and fire, as opposed to water (19:11-20:15), John saw a new heaven and a new earth, one in which there was no longer any sea. The point here may not be literally that the oceans will somehow cease to exist, but it at least means that the chaotic nature of the waters will no longer have to be feared. And it takes God's promise to never destroy the earth by a flood again to an even greater level because after Jesus returns, the oceans themselves will no longer be unpredictable and fearsome. They will no longer wreak havoc on humanity. Furthermore, all tears will be wiped away and there will no more death (Rev. 21:1-3).

This imagery and these promises almost seem unreal. This is why, if we're honest, we sometimes still have lingering concerns as to whether things could still go wrong. After all, Noah came off the ark with a clean slate and a new start, yet things still went south once the grapes in his vineyard were ripe for winemaking. How can we be so sure there might not be a possible relapse in eternity? What if Adam 2.0 becomes Adam 1.0, and we wake up back in a broken creation?

The answer to these concerns is found in Christ himself. Not any man, but God the incarnate Son will establish a new heaven and new earth, standing as the intermediary king who will merge heaven's address with the earth itself. Jesus, the God-man, is a perfect man who is also God—and God never sins. And just as no flood swept through heaven to judge its residents, so will there never be any sin or judgment when heaven and earth become one. The full righteousness of heaven will be expressed on the earth, thereby eliminating any need for judgment to be enacted.

No sea in turmoil, no humanity bogged down in corruption, no floods to overtake sinners.

WHEN JUDGMENT CEASES

We all know that floods are not pleasant occurrences. They destroy property. Worse—they take lives. They leave a huge amount of destruction in their wake. They remind us that nature is in disarray, and that things are not as they should be. Theologically, floods are illustrations of the conflict that still exists between God and mankind outside of Christ. Nevertheless, the good news is that there will never be another worldwide flood to wash away sinful humanity. More than that, we're assured that one day when Christ returns to save his people and enact final judgment, he will take away all chaos.

There will be no more sea, no more tears, no more heartbreak, and no more funerals. Creation will be renewed and those who take refuge in the divine ark known as Christ will embark into eternity with forgiveness, resurrection, and a new earth immune to any curses. As Matt Carter and Halim Suh remind us:

> [T]he surging waters were actually salvation for some and death for others. In the biblical storyline, the reality of salvation through judgment will be seen most gloriously in the cross of Jesus Christ. As Jesus was judged on the cross for our sins, we were being saved. Salvation came to us through the very instrument by which death came to Jesus. God judges sin and wickedness, but He brings salvation out of this judgment.[19]

One day, we won't scramble around like Noah, hoping to avoid leaving sin's stain on the world once again. Instead, we will look to King Jesus, whose eternal reign will never be challenged, and who will defeat sin permanently.

DISCUSSION

List a few truths you learned in this chapter that you'd not seen in Scripture before.
How do these truths apply to your life?
Why are these truths important to share with others?

3
MELCHIZEDEK

We are all tempted as consumers to be on the lookout for items that are "new and improved." Our eyes are often fixed on appliances that have more high-tech capacities, cars loaded with luxurious accessories, houses built with energy-efficient features, or cell phones with the latest upgrades. But we know from experience that cutting-edge updates do not always match their promotional hype. Newer is not always better.

At the same time, the possibility of occasional letdowns does not discourage us from taking advantage of significant leaps in technology. We know that general advances in science and industry do lead to life-changing inventions. An automobile is better than a horse and buggy, steel-toed work boots provide much more support and protection than primitive sandals, a phone is a much quicker way to contact someone than the pony express, and surgery today is much more bearable than in centuries past. So, while the promise of life-changing advances deserves a certain level of scrutiny, there are many instances where the claims are, in fact, true.

A TALE OF TWO COVENANTS

The major transition from the Old Mosaic Covenant established with Israel to the new covenant that was ratified by Christ is a similar development. Under the old agreement, the Jewish people were admonished to guard their own hearts by instilling the Law into their lives through devoted love for the Lord and obedience to his commands (Deut. 6:1-3, 20-25; 10:15-17). More specifically, it required certain obligations on Israel's part so that the Lord's provision could be experienced, whether it be fruitful harvests, communal peace in the land of Canaan, or victory over military enemies. If the covenant's stipulations were violated, the Lord promised to bring curses upon Israel as a means of judgment. This covenant was actually a gift, then, because it was grounded in an act of grace that the Lord bestowed to an undeserving party. Israel didn't "earn" the right to become God's people. Yet some of its promises were predicated on Israel's willingness to follow the Lord's instructions. And if, and when, they chose to defy his commands, there were prescribed means of divine discipline that they would receive. Unfortunately, even with God's grace and instruction, Israel was often as spiritually rebellious as the nations around them.

Ironically, this disconnect between the Lord's faithfulness to Israel and her refusal to keep her end of the Mosaic agreement is what opened the door for something spectacular. Another covenant was coming that would address these moral failings. It would show that while Israel meant her failings for evil, God actually intended them for a greater good. Israel's failure to keep her end of the covenantal bargain would not be the last word because the Lord would actually change his people by writing the Law on their very hearts (Jer. 31:33). This is not to say that this new covenant was contrary to or odds with the old one. Indeed, they both served divine purposes because they established various means whereby the Lord could have a redemptive relationship with his people. Nevertheless, it proved to be innovative and far better; similar to moving from a rotary phone to whatever the phone of the future will be (which we may not even see in our lifetimes). It did this by showing that the Lord would be faithful to use his chosen people as a channel for redeeming other peoples. Despite Israel's national failures, the expectations of a new covenant would fulfill Israel's hopes of being the vehicle by which God would bring redemption to the entire world. And this is where Christ arrives on the scene. Jesus's mission was to seal the deal—he himself would bring redemption to God's people, fulfilling the old promise and becoming the conduit of salvation for Israel and the nations.

No doubt, this was a hallmark moment in the unfolding of the biblical story. This is why the NT spends quite a bit of time discussing various parameters of the covenant that Jesus established. Here, though, we want to examine one particular feature of this better agreement—a key comparison that the book of Hebrews makes between Jesus and a man named Melchizedek who is only briefly mentioned in the OT. Melchizedek's ancient role as a priest and king carries serious overtones that directly relate to Christ as the mediator of the new covenant. How this is the case is our concern in this chapter. Let's begin our journey by looking at who Melchizedek was.

THE STORY OF MELCHIZEDEK

This mysterious figure is only mentioned twice in the OT, once in an encounter with Abraham, and later in a brief discussion in Psalm 110. From these accounts, two major features emerge. One is that Melchizedek apparently fulfilled roles that were similar to those held by later Levitical priests and Davidic kings. And the other is his place of origin, which for all accounts is unknown. Together, these factors serve as links in a chain that the author of Hebrews (AOH) later uses in the NT to describe how Jesus is a kind of Melchizedekian kingly-priest.

1. Who Was Melchizedek?

This shadowy character initially comes on the scene in the Book of Genesis. When he is introduced, we first see that his name might be more like a title. The word itself is a combination the word *melek*, which means king, and *tsedeq*, meaning righteous or righteousness—something like "righteous king." Simple enough. But an immediate question pops up. Is this term a royal designation (like "president") or his actual personal name (like "Bill")? This concern has vexed Bible scholars, because simply knowing what the conjoined words mean does not immediately resolve the matter. More detailed information about the words' ancient Semitic background reveals a variety of options. For example, some scholars have pointed out that the suffix which is combined with king, *malki*, (or melchi) can be possessive and be translated as "my king" or possibly serve as another form meaning "king of."[20] So the full word could be rendered "the king of righteousness," "zedek is my king," or "my king is just."[21] And again, any of these options could be understood as a title or name.

Likewise, along with the multiple options for translating the name are its comparative uses in other contexts. Some bring up the fact that in various ancient new covenant writings, both the words for "king" and "righteousness" are used on occasion as divine titles. We even see instances of this in the OT itself. In passages like Isaiah 46:17 alludes to God as my king. In Ezra 10:31, it refers to the LORD as my king.[22] Others counter with the argument that it can still function theoretically as a real name because we do read about an ancient king named Adoni-zedek in the days of Joshua (Josh. 10:1, 3).[23] This discussion aside, we do know that by the time we reach the days of the NT, the title-name Melchizedek was understood at least to mean "king of righteousness." Whether it was his actual name or just a title of royalty, this is the only word we have to clue us in on his identity.

Along with his name, we are also told that Melchizedek was a priest and king—two titles that do not usually go together. In fact, in the later development of Israel's history as a nation, we discover that these two offices were always distinct. Kings were never commissioned to be priests nor priests being chosen to be kings.[24] Nevertheless, Genesis ascribes both functions to this man. He is first called a king of Salem (Gen. 14:18a), which most likely is an abbreviated form of the word "Jerusalem." This deduction is partly based on another reference in Psalm 76:2 where the author, Asaph, alludes to Salem in relationship to Mount Zion in Judah.[25] "Salem" also derives from the same word family as shalom, meaning "peace." The other eye-catcher is that Melchizedek is identified as a priest of the most-high God (Gen. 14:18c). Two items are of interest here. First, no specific priest of any tribal deity has been mentioned yet in the OT story. Surely there were many during that time who served in all kinds of false religions, but none are spoken of at this point. We do see certain people performing what we might call early priestly acts like performing sacrifices in worship of the Lord (e.g., Cain, Abel, Noah, Job [if he lived before Melchizedek]). But here we have a *direct reference* to one. Second, he is a priest of God (El) the most-high—the same God that Abraham worshipped.

This connection is important because it's the basis upon which these two figures' stories intersect. The most-high God whom Melchizedek serves was the same one that calls, guides, and blesses Abraham. He is "the God (El) who sees" when intervening on Hagar's behalf (Gen. 16:13); "the Almighty God" who later reveals himself to Abraham to seal his covenantal agreement with him in a sacred ritual of sacrifice (Gen. 17:1); and "the eternal God" who provides for Abraham in his interactions with the King Abimelech (Gen. 21:33). So, we see that the Lord who chose Abraham to be his special benefactor is the same one who Melchizedek serves as some sort of priest. When such a thought sinks in, we should consider the fact that for Abraham, coming across a kingly-priest of the same God he worshipped must have been mind-blowing.

2. Melchizedek's Encounter with Abraham

At this point, a brief backstory is in order so we can understand the reason for their encounter. Melchizedek and Abraham met on the heels of Abraham's rescue mission to save his nephew Lot (Gen. 14:1-16). This story transpires early on in Abraham's sojourn through Canaan. We read that Lot chose to follow his uncle when the Lord called him to leave his family in Haran. Then after their initial travels through the land of Canaan and Egypt, they gradually made their way north again. By this time, their flocks and resources had grown to such an extent that they needed to part ways. Abraham (he was still Abram at this point) consulted with Lot on what to do. He graciously allowed Lot be the first to decide which direction he would take his caravan, and then Abraham promised that he would lead his group in the opposite way. Lot looked to the east and was so impressed with the terrain that he ventured to the valley of the Jordan and even made his way toward the city of Sodom. Abraham subsequently kept his word by settling in the region of Hebron.

Sometime after this departure, the regions of Sodom and Gomorrah engaged in a massive war. For reasons not mentioned, these two cities had pledged some sort of allegiance to a King of Elam named Chedorlaomer.[26] Their devotion had lasted for twelve years, but now in the thirteenth year, they decided to revolt. They prepared to stand their ground by making further alliances with three other regional kings who were sympathetic to their cause. Not to be outdone, Chedorlaomer also made a confederate union with three other Mesopotamian monarchs to march across the territories of these five rival kingdoms. All of these alliances led to what is known as the war of the nine kings (not to be confused with the battle of the five armies in *The Hobbit*). The early battles proved to be devastating as Chedorlaomer and his allies for all practical purposes wiped out a flurry of tribes as they made their way across the regions, conquering everything in their path. The invasions finally came to a head with a showdown between all nine kings in a valley called Siddim, which was southwest of the Salt Sea (Dead Sea). This region is described as having numerous tar pits, which proved to be disastrous. Chedorlaomer's team won the day with some of the opposing kings falling to their doom in these pits and the remaining forces fleeing to the mountains (Gen. 14:10). Afterwards, as was a custom following wars, the victors took the spoils of the defeated cities, including captives. It's here that Lot, who was a resident of Sodom, was taken as a prisoner.

Now, when invaders are nearby, people usually warn others who are unaware. One such person, who is unidentified, escaped potential capture and made his way to the oaks of Mamre in Hebron where Abraham was staying. Apparently, he had made inroads with an Amorite named Mamre, as well as his two brothers Eshcol and Aner. The informant let him know what had happened to his nephew and, in response, Abraham made a plan to save him.[27] He summoned all of his trained men who had been born to families in his camp, and it's implied that the three Amorite brothers offered their aid (Gen. 14:24). Abraham and his forces began tracking the Mesopotamian armies north. They finally caught up with them in the region of Dan, which was some 125 miles away from Mamre. Abraham knew he was vastly outnumbered, which would make the element of surprise a key to victory. So, he divided his men into groups and pounced on the enemy at night. The stealth approach worked; they soundly defeated their foes, chasing them all the way to Hobah, which was another fifty miles north of Dan. Abraham then freed Lot, regained all his possessions, and liberated the prisoners.

It was here on the cusp of this great victory that Abraham was greeted first by the King of Sodom and then by the kingly-priest, Melchizedek. They met in the valley of Shaveh (the King's Valley), which was just south of Jerusalem, or Salem. Being king of that region, Melchizedek welcomed Abraham with standard Middle Eastern hospitality by offering him bread and wine. Likewise, as a priest, Melchizedek announced a blessing on Abraham because he served the most-high God and praised Him for giving Abraham victory over his enemies (Gen 14:19-20). Abraham responded in kind by giving Melchizedek a tenth of all he had gathered in his rescue mission. The King of Sodom demanded to have his people returned to his kingdom, but was willing to let Abraham have all the spoils. Abraham swore an oath that he would not keep anything from the king except for the shares that were earned by his Amorite allies. In short, Abraham didn't want the King of Sodom to think that he had made him prosperous instead of the Lord. So, the initial point of the Melchizedek story is his role as a foil to the kingdom of Sodom. He blessed Abraham and asked for nothing, but still received a gift (a tithe) just the same.[28] Yet the king of Sodom immediately made demands, and Abraham had to act quickly so the Lord's provision would not be attributed to another source.

3. The Significance of Melchizedek and the Davidic Kings

One would think that such a significant meeting with Abraham would warrant more accounts about the life and times of Melchizedek. However, this is not the case. As we have already mentioned, he only comes up twice in the OT, once in Genesis 14, as we have seen, and centuries later in Psalm 110. In the Psalm, King David prophesies about a figure whom he identifies as the Lord (or "my lord"). He ascribes this title to him because he sees this "Lord" as being greater than he is because he shares equality with God himself. David's declaration that "the LORD (God) said to my Lord (one greater than David or any of his progeny)" seems to imply that this is a conversation in which David is a spectator, not a contributor. David says that the LORD said that he wanted the Lord to sit at his right hand until all of his enemies were made into a footstool (Psalm 110:1a-b). Stated another way, this figure (who we later come to know as the Messiah), was being given a supreme position of authority at God's throne and in time, his rule would become all-encompassing because in the end, there will be no enemies left to resist him. They will become an ottoman upon which he will rest his feet.[29] David then fleshes out this agreement with several stanzas expressing God's devotion to his anointed ruler. He will enable the

Messiah to rule in the midst of his opponents. The people will freely and gladly submit to his rule from their youth. The Lord even swears an oath to illustrate his unrelenting commitment. This guarantees that the Lord's anointed will destroy all rival kings, judge the nations, and lift up his head in glorious victory.

All of these claims are important, especially because they echo the original implications of the covenant that the Lord made with David. The merging of heavenly authority, which is eternal, with the scepter stretching from Zion (Ps. 110:2a) harmonizes well with the Lord's promise that a Davidic descendant will reign on Israel's throne forever. But along with all of these claims, David mentions a new role that this Messianic ruler will fill. Not only will he be a proper heir who comes from heaven with God's authority to rule the nations. He will also have a priestly role similar to the order of—you guessed it—Melchizedek. But how could Jesus possibly be like this ancient OT figure? These are excellent questions and fortunately the Psalm provides three major parallels.

First, it says the Lord's *king* will be a priest. This, again, is unprecedented. It marks a new transition in the story of redemption because OT regulations forbad anyone from serving in both venues. Remember it was this rule that got Israel's first king, Saul, into trouble. He tried to offer a sacrifice before a battle that only Samuel was authorized to make. Yet in this Psalm, David declared that his Lord was going to have double duty; he would rightfully serve as Israel's king as well as their priest. Second, David's Lord would not simply be another Levitical priest. He would follow in Melchizedek's footsteps by serving in a priestly office that was distinct from the one held by Aaron and the Levites. And thirdly, David quotes God as saying that his Lord will be a Melchizedekian priest *forever*. The point here is just as Melchizedek's family tree is unknown, so will Christ's priesthood be untraceable because of its uniqueness. In fact, while the Levites could only serve in accordance with "their generations," David says the Messiah will be a priest indefinitely because his reign will never end.

THE STORY OF THE LEVITICAL PRIESTHOOD

Now at this juncture, we might be tempted to dive right into the NT and begin our search for the connections between Jesus and Melchizedek. However, this would be premature. Jumping ahead too quickly overlooks one more important piece of the puzzle. Before we can grasp the parallels that the NT makes, we must briefly assess the role of the Levitical (Aaronic) priesthood. The reason this is important is because Psalm 110's link between David's Lord (Christ) and Melchizedek creates a bit of a dilemma. How can he be a priest who serves Israel if he is like Melchizedek as opposed to the Levites? It was only Aaron's descendants who could potentially serve as priestly mediators on behalf of the nation under the Mosaic economy. If David thought a future king would serve as some kind of priest, he would have to do so under the guidelines of some other covenant. And we cannot understand this point fully unless we first summarize who the Levitical priests were as well as how their duties contrast with those of Melchizedek.

1. The Establishment of the Levitical Priesthood

The role of a priest became an intricate part of Israel's life as a nation after the Exodus event. During their subsequent journey to Canaan, the people held a ceremonial gathering in the region of Mount Sinai where they received a constitution from the Lord as his newly-created nation. Because Moses, their leader, served as the initial mediating agent, we know this agreement today as the Mosaic covenant, or the Law. It entailed various rules for how the nation was to behave, as well as certain instructions for a new order of priests. This special office became known as the *Levitical* priesthood because it was delegated to Moses's older brother Aaron (Ex. 28:1-3) and his descendants who were all from the tribe of Levi. Levi was the third son born to Jacob and his first wife Leah. He had three sons, Gershon (Gershom), Kohath, and Merari; each of their descendants having roles to play. Yet Aaron's line, which was from Kohath's side of the Levitical family, had the commission to oversee the required animal sacrifices and incense in the soon-to-be-built Tabernacle, and later in the temple.

2. The Duties of the Priesthood

The Levites who qualified to serve as priests had an assortment of duties, but we can divide them into two broad categories. One set of tasks was *custodial* in nature. Here the priests were called to take care of the designated sacred space of worship and sacrifice. They were, in a sense, glorified security. This entailed constant care of the sacred furnishings, the oversight of the various offerings made on behalf of people, and moving the Tabernacle from place to place as Israel made its way to Canaan. There were even special responsibilities that the Levitical High Priest had to fulfill such as offering a sacrifice in the designated place of the Lord's presence (the Holy of Holies) once a year on the Day of Atonement. Essentially then, the priests were special go-betweens, mediating the gap between a perfect God and his imperfect people.

The other group of tasks in which priests engaged was *didactic* in nature. Along with their caretaker tasks, priests were also to be the primary experts in the Law so that they could offer moral direction and instruction to the people. They could even serve as judges (Deut. 17:8-13) in certain venues and the High Priest could offer official edicts for the people to follow. At the same time, because of these immense privileges, they were held to an extremely high standard. We see this truth, for example, in the story of Aaron's sons, Nadab and Abihu, who treated their priestly duties recklessly. Leviticus 10:1-2 says that these new priests in training offered unauthorized, or "strange," fire on the altar which the Lord had not commanded. It then says that fire immediately came from the Lord's presence and consumed them. And while this appears extreme at face value, the fact was that if the guardians of the Lord's presence acted trivially, then the people might do the same.

Moreover, keep in mind that the Levitical priesthood was instituted solely to function under the terms of the Mosaic economy. The priests came from a certain tribe. They followed the regulated sacrifices that the Law required. They offered direction and guidance that could bring covenantal blessings if followed and curses if ignored. Yet in contrast to these Levites, Melchizedek was a priestly king of Salem who didn't serve under any of these restrictions. His ministry was in a different time and consequently didn't entail the same kind of Israel-centric qualifications or obligations. One could say that their priestly roles were tied to their different objectives. Melchizedek was a king who served the city of Salem while the Levites were priests who existed only because of the requirements that the Mosaic covenant stipulated. And this point is exactly what gives us the proper angle to keep in mind as we approach the NT's descriptions of Christ as a priest.

JESUS AS A PRIEST IN THE GOSPELS

If we want to see the connections that the NT makes between Jesus and priestly activity, a good place to start is with the Gospel accounts of his earthly ministry. When we do this, we notice all kinds of priestly features that Jesus exhibited during his tenure throughout Israel. Sometimes his actions reflected many of those performed by the Levitical priests. Others moved beyond, or even transcended them. This shows us that the Gospels contain a bit of tension. On the one hand, they at times can portray Jesus as a priest comparable to the Levites. On the other hand, though, any similarities shouldn't be misconstrued to mean he was just another Levitical priest. As we shall see, some things that Jesus claimed and did actually highlighted the shortcomings of the established priesthood. This is part of the reason why he spoke of another covenant that he had come to ratify because it entailed various tasks no mere Levite could fulfill. In essence Jesus was claiming by word and deed that the Levitical office was going out of business because a new priest was in town. Moreover, the ways in which the Gospels describe this transition form the perfect backdrop for understanding some of the reasons why the AOH compares Jesus, as a new priest, to Melchizedek.

1. Jesus Has More Authority than Israel's Priests

One major theme that pops up occasionally in the Gospels is how Jesus understood his role as Messiah in light of priestly duties. A clear example of this can be seen an interchange he had with some Pharisees after his disciples were accused of breaking a Sabbath regulation. In this account, which we find in all of the Synoptic Gospels (Matt. 12:1-8; Mk. 2:23-28; Lk. 6:1-5), Jesus and his followers were walking through a grain field on the Sabbath. Being hungry, his disciples began picking heads of grain to eat and the Pharisees were nearby. They accused the disciples of desecrating the Sabbath because their actions were considered a breach of rabbinic code. While handpicking grain was not technically a Sabbath violation, the Law did forbid using a sickle for harvesting on the Sabbath (Lev. 19:9-10; Deut. 23:25). So, their complaint was probably based on an established Jewish tradition that equated plucking with reaping.[30]

Jesus responds to their charge by providing two major comparisons. He first recounts the story of David when he was on the run from King Saul. He was permitted by the priest Ahimelech to have some of the sacred showbread from the furnished table in the tabernacle, which was restricted to the priests only. Now by the letter of the law, this was unacceptable. But it was seen as permissible because of who David was as the anointed soon-to-be king of Israel. Then as a follow up, Jesus mentions the fact that some of the biggest Sabbath violators were the priests themselves. They were engaged in all kinds of vocational activity on the Sabbath. Yet because of who they were as God's delegated servants in the tabernacle, their work, in a sense, took precedence over numerous Sabbath restrictions.

From here, Jesus then makes a final and important point. He claims that something greater than the Temple and the Sabbath was in their midst.

Jesus was saying that just as David's immediate need for food trumped the technical restrictions of the showbread and the priestly service in the Temple, so likewise was he greater than the Sabbath itself and by implication, the priests and David too. This was quite a startling claim. The Pharisees were in the presence of an authority that far surpassed the Davidic and priestly ones they were willing to accept. And since this was true, it also meant that the role of the Levitical priests was on borrowed time. The Messiah had far greater clout and power.

2. Jesus Performed Priestly Acts During His Ministry

Along with his authority, the Gospels also describe certain acts that Jesus performed with strong priestly overtones. Some of them even resemble what Levitical priests often did on Israel's behalf quite well. We know, for instance, that the Levitical priests often interceded on behalf of the people so the Lord would grant blessings and forgiveness (2 Chron. 30:27). We see Jesus doing the very same thing on numerous occasions. He gave thanks to God when he performed certain miracles like the feeding of the multitudes (Mk. 6:41; Lk. 9:16). On the night of his betrayal, amidst all of his agony and the cup that was being put before him, he graciously interceded for his disciples because of what they were about to face and even prayed for all who believe in him (Jn 17). Today we even call this his "high priestly" prayer. Then after his resurrection, Luke and John record Jesus invoking blessings on his disciples before departing, which was also something the priests were known for doing (cf., Num. 6:22-27; Lk. 24:50; Jn. 20:19).

Added to these resemblances are other features that Jesus expressed which made him to stand head and shoulders above the Levites. One critical example was his ability to eliminate the entire clean/unclean dilemma, which was intrinsic to the Mosaic code. Specifically, there were numerous restrictions excluding the Israelites from being able to come into the Lord's tabernacle (or temple) presence. Anything that was an external expression of the curse upon creation such as death, deformity, or decay automatically disqualified one from being able to approach the sacred space of the Lord, which again was guarded by the priests. Nevertheless, we see Jesus exercising authority that overcame this problem. He could come into contact with a corpse, engage someone with a physical deformity, or touch a leper without becoming ceremonially defiled. On top of that feat, his word or touch actually restored (or resurrected) anyone who suffered from these calamities. This is why on occasions when Jesus healed a leper, he didn't become unclean as the Law prescribed (Lev. 5:3). Instead lepers were healed as well as cleansed, and then to top it off, they sometimes were instructed to go show themselves to a priest and offer a gift that Moses required (Lev. 13-14). This is intriguing because under the Law, Levitical priests could only provide a ceremonial diagnosis. They could declare someone unclean if they were leprous and merely acknowledge that someone was clean if they recovered from leprosy. But Jesus was radically different. He offered a cure to the unclean stigma without becoming unclean himself. In fact, it's entirely possible that one of the reasons many priests later embraced him as Israel's Messiah was because his miraculous healings testified to his power (Acts 6:7).

Another stand-alone feat that distinguished Jesus as a unique priest was his ability to provide direct access into the Lord's presence. This was unprecedented because originally the Levitical priests were the only ones who could directly approach the Lord in the sacred space of the tabernacle or temple. And even when they did, it was still heavily restricted. The priests of Aaron served in the outer area known as the Holy Place and the high priest could only enter the room where the Ark of the Covenant was present (the Holy of Holies) once a year. Obviously no one could just trot into the sacred presence without suffering dire consequences. Added to this role were the responsibilities of overseeing the assortment of sacrifices that God had prescribed in the Law.

However, Christ actually combines the priestly duties, something no Levite could ever do. Instead of extending a lamb, bull, turtle dove, or other acceptable offering on the altar of sacrifice for one's own personal forgiveness, he offered himself as a sacrifice for the sins of others. This act put the previous Levitical system completely on ice. This is illustrated beautifully in the Gospels where it's said that upon Jesus's death, the veil was torn in two—the one separating the sacred space of the Lord's presence in the Temple from the other courts in which the priests and people traversed. This meant that the point of convergence between heaven and earth was no longer the mercy seat on the Ark of the Covenant in the Jewish temple. It was now the Jewish Messiah himself who had atoned for the sins of the world and would ultimately be resurrected to ensure that no second sacrifice would ever be required. Thus, Jesus acted as a different kind of priest because instead of offering a sacrifice, he became one himself. Instead of guarding the Lord's presence, he opened wide the doors to heaven's throne room itself.

JESUS AS A PRIEST LIKE MELCHIZEDEK

So far, we have seen some of the ways in which the Gospels portray Jesus as a new kind of priest who rivals the role of the Levites and even the high priest himself. Still, the Gospels, Acts, nor any of the other NT writings take the discussion further by applying the subject of Melchizedek to the mix except for the Book of Hebrews. In this epistle, the author writes to an audience of believers concerning the supremacy of Christ and how the covenant he ratified abolishes the original Mosaic one. It appears that his main motivation is to assure an audience who was considering abandoning their faith and reverting back into some form of Judaism.[31]

Next, the AOH uses this comparison to show his readers the vanity of reverting back to Judaism, because the old covenant had transitioned to new covenant fulfillment. To apostatize or fall away would be the greatest of tragedies, because it would mean one was returning to a system that no longer was in effect. Finding salvation in the Law would be like trying to make a living with Monopoly money—the currency has no real value. The author points out that Jesus is a new high priest of a new kind of covenant. As opposed to being a Levitical priest who served on the Law's watch, Jesus is now a different kind of priest who reflects the ancient role of Melchizedek.[32] Let's explore a few ways that this works out.

1. Melchizedek and Jesus Are Greater than Abraham and the Levites (Heb. 6:19-7:10)

The initial link that the AOH makes between Jesus as a priest and Melchizedek is that they both possess a special kind of rank or authority.

This point emerges when the AOH mentions Abraham. He claims that if the readers remain faithful and patiently endure hardship, they will be following in the footsteps of Abraham who also waited for the Lord to fulfill his promises in his day. Just as the Lord made an oath to reward Abraham, these early believers could be assured of their vindication, because Jesus became their forerunner and is now their advocate-priest similar to the "order of Melchizedek."

From here, the AOH then recounts the basic parameters of the story about Melchizedek to build a case regarding the superiority of Christ's priesthood over the Levites'. He starts by highlighting the fact that after his military victory, Abraham came into contact with Melchizedek who, again, was a king and a priest. But unlike other ancient kings and priests, we are given no record of his family history or genealogical background. The AOH even says we are unaware of his time of birth or even death.[33] Even so, Abraham still gave a tithe of his spoils from his recent battle to Melchizedek. And in response, he imparted a blessing to Abraham.

Similarly, the AOH reminds his readers that Levitical priests were the later recipients of tithes and offerings from the other eleven tribes of Israel thereby making them distinct from the rest of the nation. The line of logic goes like this. Even though the Levites were distinct from Israel because they were the chosen tribe for priestly duties, they were still, in a sense, subordinate to Abraham as their alpha patriarch. Yet Abraham showed deference to Melchizedek by offering tithes to him. Furthermore, because all the tribes of Israel, including Levi, were ultimately the product of Abraham's promised seed, they were also subordinate to Melchizedek too. Consequently, if Jesus functioned as a supreme prototype of Melchizedek (whoever this figure was), then by default he is greater than Abraham as well as the Levites. He is the greatest, bar none.

2. Jesus Is a Priest of a Better Covenant (Heb. 7:11-8:13)

The AOH also contends that Christ's priestly actions are far greater than the Levites' actions. Or put another way, the covenant that he established supersedes any service that old covenant priests ever offered. This argument begins to take shape once the AOH observes that Jesus didn't qualify to be a priest because he came from the wrong tribe (Judah rather than Levi). One might think this put the Lord on the horns of a dilemma since Jesus would be violating a non-negotiable qualification to be a priest. Yet the AOH claims that this is good news because humanity didn't need another Levitical priest. There were just too many concerns in the Mosaic economy that needed attention. One was that neither Aaron nor his descendants could ever achieve a final settlement between man and God. The reason being that while the prescribed sacrifices that they offered brought effectual atonement, the results were never permanent.

Likewise, even the priests themselves were sinners in need of forgiveness. Sometimes they were so corrupt that they joined Israel in all of her idolatry. And no matter what their spiritual disposition, all priests eventually died, which meant there was always a need for new ones to serve in every generation. Finally, the Levites could only administer the ramifications of the Mosaic covenant, which did temporarily remedy one's status of guilt, but never transformed the deeper condition of the human heart.

Now in contrast, the AOH shows how Christ shored up all of these blind spots and Melchizedek is a key component. Essentially the AOH appeals to Psalm 110's connection between Melchizedek as a priestly king and the expected Messiah who would perpetuate the Lord's kingdom. The overall point that the AOH makes is that Christ fulfills this hope by ratifying a new covenant. For instance, as opposed to the unending litany of old covenant sacrifices, Christ offered one sacrifice for all time. Once he did, its benefits included cleansing from the guilt of sin as well as an inward transformation of the heart.

Furthermore, Jesus has no need of any successors because his ministry is unending and his sacrifice was solely vicarious in nature because there was no need to atone for his own sin. So just as Melchizedek was a king priest who functioned outside all of the Levitical rules, Christ is now the Davidic king who also serves as a High Priest of a covenant that achieved goals which the Law was never intended to attain. Christ shocked the world by crossing all of the Mosaic boundaries and bringing the ancient prophecy of Psalm 110 to a fitting end. Just as Melchizedek was a mysterious kingly priest whose origins were unknown, so David's God would delegate his Messiah to be both the divine king and priest for his people forever. Thus, this transition is truly an instance where newer is better.

NEWER IS BETTER

In the case of Jesus, newer really is better. And this is not only true for this chapter. Every chapter in this book shows that this is an inescapable truth of Scripture. Jesus didn't simply eradicate some old dusty blueprint left in God's eternal attic. Instead, he shows us that the old covenant was only one part of a bigger story. The Law was never meant to remedy everything that is wrong with humanity. That is why the incarnation had to happen. The arc of history bends toward Jesus. Indeed, he is the fulfillment of every promise for redemption that God made, as well as the climax to which OT stories point--even short ones that seem random and insignificant on their own.

DISCUSSION

List a few truths you learned in this chapter that you'd not seen in Scripture before.

How do these truths apply to your life?

Why are these truths important to share with others?

4
MOSES

We are all familiar with stories in which a leadership vacuum is created when young upstarts cannot fill the shoes of their predecessors. Sometimes this is because a former leader is so beloved that the people just cannot transfer their affection to the new leader. Other times it occurs simply because a young successor just does not have the same skills or competence as the predecessor. In any case, we see this kind of ordeal in many contexts. It happens in the development of powerful empires where kings die and their heirs are not able to hold the kingdom together. It can emerge within families when sons or daughters cannot live up to standards that their parents set because of their prestige or achievements. It happens when the young, hip pastor tries to steer an established church in a new direction. It can even come up in sports, when an influential coach develops a reputation that the following one can never match. But in some cases, leaders actually do prove themselves to be even more effective than the ones before them.

The best example is when the success of one leader is based on the foundation laid by a previous one. Sometimes, the best indicator of a leader's influence is the ability to successfully hand off the role to another.

We see this exemplified in the Bible on numerous occasions. King David collected all the materials for building the Temple so that when his son Solomon took the throne, he could begin its construction immediately. The prophet Elijah's faithfulness during a volatile time of Israel's history set a precedent for his student Elisha, who asked for a double portion of his teacher's power. And the apostle Paul spoke of how the things he had taught his students, like Timothy, should be shared with others so that they would be equipped to pass the faith on to future generations. Yet the most significant time where a previous leader's accomplishments were far surpassed by a later one occurred when Jesus came to deliver Israel in a significantly different way than Moses had in the nation's earlier history.

GOD, MOSES, AND FREEDOM

Moses is one of the most beloved figures in Israel's history. He was the reluctant leader who led the people out of Egypt after they had suffered in slavery for centuries. He was the one who then led them to the region of Sinai where he served as their mediator when the Lord ratified a covenant with them. He was the one who stood beside them when most of the nation refused to enter the Promised Land and had to traverse the Sinai wilderness for a forty-year internal as punishment. In many ways, he was the premiere leader of Israel even with all his faults. His character became so respected that even Scripture itself testifies that Moses was the humblest man of his day (Num. 12:3).

So, humanly speaking, he had every reason to be cocky. He was the one who was called by God in the miraculous burning bush account. He was the one who later led Israel out of Egypt after the ten plagues.

He alone was able to commune with the Lord atop Mount Sinai, to the extent that the Lord's glory literally shone off of his face so greatly that he was required to wear a veil. And he was the one with whom the Lord spoke directly as opposed to using visions or dreams. Yet he was so overwhelmed with God's greatness and his own frailty that his pride never got the best of him.

1. Moses's Call to Serve the Lord

Moses's story began with humble means because of the dire times in which he was born. He was part of a Hebrew family who lived at the time when a Pharaoh of Egypt had not only enslaved the Hebrews, but had issued a death sentence upon all baby Hebrew boys (Ex. 1). Afraid for their son's life, Moses's parents put him in a basket and sent him down the Nile River, in desperate hopes that he would land in a safer place. No doubt, anywhere seemed better than home. Moses, of course, ended up at what seemed to be the worst possible place: in the hands of the Pharaoh's daughter. His daughter, however, felt compassion for Moses and adopted him into the royal family. In the Lord's providence, Moses went from being born with a death sentence to living in a palace with his would-be executioner (Ex. 2:1-10).

From here, the biblical story jumps forward to Moses as a grown man. Aware of his real heritage, he began observing the hardships that his people were enduring when one day he witnessed an Egyptian beating a Hebrew slave. Moses became so furious that he murdered the Egyptian and buried him in the sand. Then later, he saw two Hebrews in a squabble. To his chagrin, when he demanded that they stop fighting, one of them claimed that he no right to correct them. He asked if Moses would kill one of them to settle the matter, as he did earlier with the bully Egyptian. Moses knew in that moment that his sin was no secret, as he apparently assumed. What made matters worse is that Pharaoh was informed of the matter as well, and he issued (yet another) death sentence on Moses (Ex. 2:11-15).

From here, Moses fled Egypt out of fear, leaving his oppressed kinsmen behind. But God was not done with him or Israel. Eventually he remembered the covenant he had made with the people, which meant he was going to intervene in history precisely because of the promises he had originally made with Abraham (Ex. 2:23). And the first step was to summon a leader to guide the people out of Egypt--enter Moses back on the scene.

We read in Exodus 3 that God appeared to him in the famous burning bush, telling him to return to Egypt. Moses initially posed many objections and excuses. Yet the Lord told him that he had nothing to fear because not only would he protect him when he returned. He would also enable Moses to lead the Hebrews out of slavery into the Promised Land (Ex. 3:8-10). Then, the next scene is so powerful that it sends a shockwave through the rest of history:

> Then Moses asked God, "If I go to the Israelites and say to them, 'The God of your fathers has sent me to you,' and they ask me, 'What is his name?' what should I tell them?" God replied to Moses, "I AM WHO I AM. This is what you are to say to the Israelites: I AM has sent me to you." God also said to Moses, "Say this to the Israelites: The Lord, the God of your fathers, the God of Abraham, the God of Isaac, and the God of Jacob, has sent me to you. This is my name forever; this is how I am to be remembered in every generation. (Ex. 3:13-15)

Notice here that when Moses asked how he could identify the Lord, his response was that "I AM WHO I AM." In other words, "There is no one like me. I am unique. I AM because nobody else IS." This came to be known as the powerful name of God that would be remembered in every generation—the name of the one who was in covenant with his people, the one who was committed to their deliverance and ultimately, their inheritance of the Promised Land.

2. Moses and the Exodus

Moses then returned to Egypt, along with his brother Aaron, so they could confront the new Pharaoh with a message from heaven—let the people of Israel go. Pharaoh refused, as the Lord predicted he would, and this led to showdown against many of the alleged Egyptian deities to which Pharaoh paid homage. We read about ten specific plagues that the Lord brought upon the Egyptian people, showing his divine power over things they thought were controlled by their own gods. However, the greatest authority the Lord could vanquish was the regal dynasty of Egypt's leader. So, he brought death on every Egyptian's firstborn, including Pharaoh's own son. Likewise, it was here where God gave instructions to Moses regarding the sacred Passover meal, wherein the people of Israel could provide a sacrificial lamb for each of their households that could serve as a means of protection from this final plague.

After this ego-crushing night, Pharaoh conceded to let Israel go free. But shortly afterwards, he was so enraged by his losses that he led his armies to chase down the Hebrews so he could slaughter them. With Pharaoh and his legions pursuing from behind with the Red Sea standing in front of them, things did not look good for Moses and the people. But instead of being overtaken by their enemies, the Lord performed the great miracle of parting the Red Sea so the people could escape. And as a final act of deliverance, the Lord let the waters crash down on the ensuing Egyptian forces. This victorious account ends with Moses and the Israelites singing a song of triumph, a song that became known as "The Song of Moses" (Ex. 15). They sang because Egypt was defeated, Israel was delivered, and the Lord was their warrior. Nothing could go wrong now, right?

Not so fast. We learn throughout the story that there was another major foe from which Israel needed deliverance—their own covenant-breaking hearts. For example, though they had been freed from slavery, it did not take long for God's people to begin grumbling and falter in their allegiance. They quickly forgot how the Lord had delivered them. They bemoaned,

> *If only we had died by the LORD's hand in the land of Egypt, when we sat by pots of meat and ate all the bread we wanted. Instead, you brought us into this wilderness to make this whole assembly die of hunger!* (Ex. 16:3; cf. 17:1-3)

They sound an awful lot like Adam and Eve here, questioning the blessings that God had provided. And just like our first parents, such doubts led Israel to all sorts of disobedience. We discover that Israel's track record throughout the rest of the Exodus account is one of consistent defiance, only with a few shining moments where Moses and a remnant of faithful believers kept their eyes on God.

Not shortly after the Red Sea victory, we read that the masses committed gross immorality and idolatry while Moses was atop Mount Sinai receiving the Law from the Lord, so that Israel could officially be his newly redeemed people. Then after being disciplined for such egregious failure, the majority of people later refused to enter the land of promise because the tribes that were already fortified there intimidated them. Moses had sent twelve spies in to the land, one representing each tribe of Israel, to case out the situation. When they returned to give a report, ten of the twelve made the tragic mistake of comparing their own might with that of the native inhabitants. They thought they were grasshoppers in the sight of the Canaanites, and no doubt, they were absolutely right. The problem was that they failed to see the situation through the eyes of faith. If they would have, they could have seen that the enemies were even smaller than grasshoppers in the Lord's sight. Only two of the twelve, Joshua and Caleb, saw things in the proper light. Yet instead of being inspired by their faith, the masses listened to the skepticism of the majority and committed one of the greatest cases of unbelief in Israel's history.

Finally, because they failed to see the fulfillment of the promise that God had made to Abraham centuries ago, they did not inherit the land. In turn, the Lord judged the nation by causing it to wander in the Middle Eastern wilderness for forty years until the majority of them died. Instead, the children, Joshua and Caleb, and a few other designated Israelites entered Canaan a generation later. Throughout this forty-year ordeal, Moses continued to serve as a faithful mediator for the people. He endured criticism, faced rebellions, and even forfeited his own privilege to enter Canaan because he lost his temper with them. By the time the dust cleared, Moses had become the most revered leader in the nation's early history.

THE ROLES OF MOSES IN THE EXODUS STORY

We can see that Moses's life is a central part of the biblical story about Israel's deliverance from Egypt. Still, a considerable challenge some can often face when studying this important OT figure is trying to put their minds around all of the various duties that Moses filled on behalf of the nation. To simply say that he was the people's "leader" is shortsighted. But if we hone in on some of the basic details of Moses's ministry, we'll uncover a few helpful details about his place in Scripture and salvation history.

First, grasping the fundamental roles in which Moses served helps one see how other books of the Pentateuch (i.e., first five books of the OT) connect to the Exodus story--those being Leviticus, Numbers, and Deuteronomy. Second, being familiar with facets of Moses's ministry can help prepare one to see many of the connections that the NT makes between Jesus, Moses, and the entire Exodus event. That being said, three roles stand out the most—prophet, deliverer, and lawgiver.

1. Prophet

One clear title that can be ascribed to Moses is that of a prophet. Throughout the OT, prophets spoke on behalf of God. Whether through words spoken or written, prophets were known for their famous line, "Thus says the Lord." Also, they were not just any Joe off the street. No one could just arbitrarily volunteer to speak for the Lord off the cuff. They had to be directly called and selectively empowered by the Spirit to prophesy (1 Sam. 19:20; 2 Chron 20:14; Ezek 11:5); be subject to God's command (Deut. 18:18-22); sometimes perform accompanying signs; and prove one's authenticity by seeing one's prophecies come to pass (1 Sam. 10:3-11; 1 Kgs. 13:5; 2 Kgs. 19:29, 20:9; Jer. 28:15-17; Ezek. 33:33).[34]

We see each of these factors in the life of Moses, beginning with his divine encounter at the burning bush where he was summoned to be God's spokesperson. The Lord revealed his plans to use Moses as Israel's new leader. But immediately feeling the gravity of such a mantle, Moses tried to counter the Lord's call with a litany of excuses as to why he was not qualified, which was something other prophets-in-training would do. Among them was the concern that the people would not hear Moses. So, the Lord promised that he would be able to perform various miracles to validate his credentials as his legitimate mouthpiece.

Moses then said that he was not an eloquent speaker. Yet the Lord again would not take no for answer. He told Moses that his brother Aaron could speak on his behalf. This created an interesting relay of communication because the Lord told Moses that he would be like a god to Pharaoh and that Aaron would be his prophet (Ex. 7:1-2). The point of this comparison was that just as Moses received the word of the Lord as a prophet, Aaron then received that message from Moses, thereby being his prophet. The way Pharaoh saw it, Moses was acting like a divine being who let his delegated spokesperson do all the talking. Thus, while Moses was actually God's prophet, Pharaoh thought Aaron was. This interaction was a direct challenge to the divine authority Pharaoh claimed to hold.

As the story continues to unfold, we continue to read of numerous occasions where Moses performed all kinds of miraculous signs and made predictions that came true. In fact, at one point later in the journey to Canaan, Moses's sister Miriam and brother Aaron questioned whether the Lord only spoke through him (Num. 12). The Lord confronted them and said that as opposed to other prophets who may receive divine messages through visions, dreams, or dark sayings, he chose to speak to Moses clearly and plainly. God spoke directly through Moses; this made him a prophet, yes, but also a sort of prototype for all other prophets.

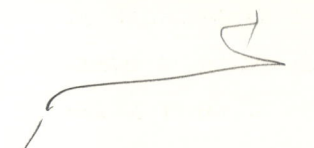

2. Deliverer

A second major role played by Moses was as a deliverer. In some ways, this was the most pertinent job that Moses had because the need for such a person is stressed immediately in the Book of Exodus. The Hebrew people were in bondage. They were beaten, whipped, and overworked, with no hope in sight. Yet even though Israel did not expect Egypt to relent, the Lord provided a person they least expected to fight for their cause. He allowed a young Hebrew baby boy to be raised in Egyptian royalty so he could eventually serve as a kind of Trojan horse. This adopted Egyptian would be chosen by the Lord to deliver their slave population. More importantly, this rescue project was the way that God would keep his promises made to Abraham centuries earlier.

This connection can be seen later when Moses is summoned to serve the Lord. He is told that he will be sent to Pharaoh so that he may bring Israel, the Lord's people, out of Egypt (Ex. 3:10). Though he will not do so in his own power—it is by his leadership that the Lord would show his might over Egypt and redeem his people. Moses delivered Israel in the sense that his answer to the Lord's call on his life was part of the means whereby Israel was rescued from the clutches of slavery.[35]

Furthermore, Moses's willingness to lead Israel went beyond just leaving the land of Egypt. There were moments where Moses had to stand in the gap as Israel's mediator before the Lord because of his or her own reckless behavior. Sometimes these moments were intense, so much so that Moses's intercession on behalf of the people was often the only thing that prevented their utter destruction. Consequently, the job of being Israel's deliverer did not stop once the beat down in Egypt was over. The people were constantly in need of someone to be their go-between because they were also in need of deliverance from their covenant-breaking hearts. And like any good leader, Moses was willing to take the lumps for his team because his top priorities were the people's spiritual well-being and God's glory..

3. Lawgiver

Finally, Scripture presents Moses as Israel's lawgiver. This responsibility emerges early on after the Exodus, when Moses is adjudicating matters among the people. He served as an elder-judge once they embarked on their long journey to the Promised Land. Eventually the responsibilities were increasing at such an alarming rate that his father-in-law advised him to delegate some of his duties to qualified elders among the people. That way, Moses could have a buffer of helpers so he would not be overwhelmed with every complaint among the masses. Then, as they approached Mount Sinai, Moses was the one who brought the first draft of Israel's Bill of Rights—the Ten Commandments. These rules served as the fundamental basis for the later drafting of the entire Law, which was Israel's official constitution as God's newly redeemed nation (cf. Ex. 20:1-17).

Collectively, all of the commands in the Law were provided so the Israelites could have a clear picture of what God expected of them.

Their conduct was to be an outflow of who they were. They were now a redeemed people who did not belong to themselves. Their everyday lives were to reflect the spiritual privileges they had been granted. And the Law was the blueprint that they were to follow so this goal could be achieved. Furthermore, Moses served as the initial emissary who distributed the Law to the people, both in its first edition (Ex. 32) and in its second (Deut. 10). Thus, Moses became the bridge between the heavenly court wherein God articulated his laws and the nation of Israel who was to be the benefactor of this ratified "Mosaic" covenant. In a sense, then, Moses's role as a lawgiver tied his other tasks of being a deliverer and prophet together—by revealing God's commandments to the people, he proclaimed God's words like a prophet and gave them an outline for how they could have deliverance from the slavery of sin.

JESUS AND THE ROLES OF MOSES

Because of the critical place Moses occupies in Israel's history, it is only fitting that the NT would have much to say about his ministry—and how Jesus parallels and even transcends his ministry. The easiest way to see this is by simply observing how Jesus replicates the actions of Moses-- he served as Israel's premiere prophet, deliverer, and lawgiver. The NT teaches that Jesus clearly fulfilled the job description for all of these tasks. And on top of that, sometimes the ways in which he performed them are described in ways that allude back to important moments of Moses's life as if Jesus was actually reliving them. Let's look at a few examples.

1. Jesus Is the Final Prophet

The prophetic office is a great place to begin considering how Moses and Jesus overlap in the biblical story. For starters, Jesus was like Moses in that he met all the criteria one would look for in a prophet. This is not to insinuate that he was merely a prophet, mind you. This was the mistake that many in Jesus's day made. He was the divine Son of God incarnate, the Messiah of Israel. At the same time, this does not mean he was failed to be the true and better prophet of Israel. Indeed, he was the ultimate prophet. As opposed to being one to whom the "Word of the Lord" came, as it did to Moses and all the other OT prophets, Jesus, as the divine Son, was the Word itself. He embodied the final word of the Father as the Savior who was sent to bring salvation to all those who believe (Jn. 1:1-2; Heb. 1:1-2).

Jesus also acted like other prophets through his words and actions. He announced woes of judgment against unrepentant sinners, while at other times he offered words of encouragement to those in need. He sometimes performed parabolic actions to illustrate a point about Israel's condition, like cursing a fig tree that bore no fruit or kicking people out of the Temple who were consumed with commerce instead of prayer and worship. Likewise, the Gospels are full of accounts where Jesus performed a multitude of miracles-- so much so that his followers asked him to be like the great prophet Elijah and call down fire from heaven (Lk. 9:52-55). Finally, Jesus predicted future events like prophets often did. Predicting his death and resurrection and the destruction of the temple in Jerusalem are the most striking examples.

Now admittedly, if we were to stop here, it would seem somewhat arbitrary to emphasize a connection with Moses specifically–after all, Jesus's prophetic actions reflect those of numerous OT prophets.

However, Jesus's greatness as a prophet is sometimes directly described as being superior to that of Moses. One great illustration of this can be found in a prophecy that Moses himself gave to Israel. In Deuteronomy 18:15-19, Moses claimed that

> "The LORD your God will raise up for you a prophet like me from among your own brothers. You must listen to him. This is what you requested from the LORD your God at Horeb on the day of the assembly when you said, 'Let us not continue to hear the voice of the LORD our God or see this great fire any longer, so that we will not die!' Then the LORD said to me, 'They have spoken well. I will raise up for them a prophet like you from among their brothers. I will put my words in his mouth, and he will tell them everything I command him. I will hold accountable whoever does not listen to my words that he speaks in my name...'"

This proclamation became quite legendary among Jews for centuries, because it represented a larger hope for a Messiah who would deliver them from their enemies and establish God's kingdom on the earth. So, when Jesus arrived on the scene and exhibited all the signs of being such a prophet, people began to wonder if he might be the one. There were times when people perceived that he was some sort of prophet (Lk. 24:19; Jn. 4:19). And at other times, people wondered if he might be the messenger of which Moses spoke (Jn. 6:14). Nevertheless, after Jesus's resurrection, the early church clearly made the connection by proclaiming that he was the Christ (anointed one and Messiah), the coming prophet that Moses had anticipated (cf., Acts 3:22, 7:37).

Even more emphatically, Moses's prediction is highlighted in the famous event at the scene of the Transfiguration. Here, Jesus took Peter, James, and John on a high mountain to let them witness his concealed majesty. He allowed them to see, if only for a moment, his divine glory. His face radiated like the sun and his clothes became brilliantly bright, similar to the way in which Moses shone after being in God's presence (Matt. 17:1-2). And then the Gospel accounts tell us something astounding. Moses and Elijah appeared to talk with Jesus. We are not told why this encounter took place or what they spoke of in detail other than they conversed about the Lord's upcoming events in Jerusalem (Lk. 9:31).[36] However, it is critical to note that Moses and Elijah were the two heavyweights among Israel's prophets, primarily because both of them were able to commune with the Lord on mountains where no one else could tread. We read in Exodus 24 and 34 that Moses conversed with the Lord as he recorded the Law, and in 1 Kings 19, Elijah encountered the Lord on a mountain as well.

Now, once again, these two greats were on a mountain—this time to convene with the Son of God. When the incredible moment ended, a cloud encompassed the disciples with a voice coming from heaven that said, "This is my beloved Son, with whom I am well-pleased. Listen to him!" What should not be missed here is that the heavenly Father did not tell the disciples to hear Elijah or Moses. We are not even privy to anything they said specifically. What Peter, James, and John are told to do is listen to the one with whom Moses and Elijah conversed. While these OT greats had heard the Lord's voice on various mountains, now they had the unique opportunity to hear the voice of God and see the face of God at the same time. This admonition from heaven coincided perfectly with what Moses had originally told Israel to do—listen to the voice of the prophet who God would send.

2. Jesus Is the Final Deliverer

The NT also identifies Jesus as the deliverer of a new Exodus. As we have seen previously, Moses was called to lead the first one so God's people, the Israelites, could escape slavery in Egypt and commence their journey to the land of Canaan. In doing so, the cruel master who was defeated was an ego-driven Pharaoh. Nevertheless, as we saw earlier, there was a more powerful dictator that plagued the lives of the Israelites—their own rebellious hearts. The people of Israel were sinners whether they were in Egypt, traveling through the Sinai wilderness, or in the Promised Land itself. So even though Moses could lead the people out of Egypt, he could not mend their spiritual brokenness. Therefore, a deliverer who could do this would far surpass Moses, and this is why the NT often describes Jesus in this way. Israel's redemption from Egypt in the Exodus became a sort of prelude to a future deliverance from Satan's kingdom and the corruption of sin. The question, though, is how the NT connects these dots.

Foundationally, Jesus's story as a new deliverer begins the same way Moses's account did, namely with a situation where God delivered him. Just as Moses was born during a time when Pharaoh felt threatened and tried to kill all of Israel's baby boys, the pagan ruler Herod likewise felt his authority jeopardized when he was told that the King of the Jews had been born (Matt. 2:1-3). He joined Pharaoh centuries later by leveling the same death sentence against all baby boys in Bethlehem and the surrounding regions. Yet just as Moses escaped in a basket that was sent down a river, Jesus was rescued when his father Joseph made an escape down into Egypt. Likewise, while baby Jesus was protected by the Lord's provision, the angel Gabriel also announced to Mary before his conception that he would deliver his people, not from a Pharaoh or even Herod, but from their sins (Matt. 1:21).

More parallels with the Exodus continue as Jesus's ministry launches. Some of them begin at Jesus's baptism where he is identified as the Father's beloved Son, which echoes the same title ascribed to Israel when Moses was summoned at the burning bush (Ex. 4:22). Afterwards, Jesus, the true Israelite, was led by the Spirit into the wilderness to be tempted by the devil. Satan tempted him with the need for food when he had been fasting for forty days. But whereas Israel complained about food and water, Jesus chose to wait patiently on his Father's provision to meet his needs. This portrayal of Jesus as being faithful where Israel failed continues throughout Matthew, Mark, and Luke, especially in light of the prophet Isaiah's contrast between Israel as a rebellious servant of the Lord as opposed to an unidentified suffering servant who serves the Lord faithfully (Isa. 52-53). Jesus is identified as this servant who endures punishment for the sake of his people; brings the acceptable year of the Lord where Israel finds deliverance from physical maladies, death, and sin; and dispenses the Spirit to his people. Jesus here is depicted as one greater than Moses because the exodus he pioneers is a serious upgrade from the first one.

The wilderness motif is also important in John's Gospel. He recounts numerous times in which Jesus claimed to meet the needs of both Jews and Gentiles just as the Lord did for Israel in their wanderings. Jesus claimed to bring healing, similar to the bronze serpent on a pole did in Moses's day when the Israelites looked upon it after being bitten by poisonous snakes (Jn. 3:14-15). He gives wells of living water to produce eternal life in those who believe (Jn. 4:13-14). He is the bread of life that has come from heaven (Jn. 6:32-33). And he is the light of the world who illumines some and blinds others (Jn. 9:5). All of these referents were provided for Israel during their wilderness wanderings--water from a rock, manna from heaven, and a pillar of fire to lead the people at night. These items become indicative of who Jesus is and what he can do for all those who believe. Going even further, John also recounts a debate Jesus had with the Jewish religious authorities where he embraced the sacred name of God, the great I AM, thus claiming authority as the one who called Moses to be Israel's deliverer (Jn. 8:58). God provided for Israel in her first Exodus, and now Jesus is the one who will provide the means for a second and greater one.

Keeping stride with this emphasis, other NT writers see Moses and the Exodus as key lenses through which we should understand Christ's work on our behalf. One prime example can be seen in the first letter Paul wrote to the Corinthians, where he claims that Israel's failures in the wilderness are recorded so that believers in Christ can learn from them and not make the same mistakes (1 Cor. 10:1-13). Paul says that just as Israel was identified with Moses in the Red Sea miracle, so likewise are followers of Jesus identified with him because they have partaken of the age to come. In fact, part of the reason we are now part of Christ's kingdom is because he serves as our Passover sacrifice that protects us from judgment (1 Cor. 5:7).

The same emphasis on the wilderness wanderings pops up in other writings, such as the Book of Jude. Here, the author admonishes his readers not to fall short in their commitment the way Israel did in the wilderness (Jd. 5). The writer of Hebrews also echoes the same sentiment by claiming that because Jesus is better than Moses by virtue of the fact that he has ratified a better covenant. Because of this new covenant, believers should not commit the same mistake as Israel did and fail to enter their eternal rest in the coming kingdom (Heb. 2-4). They should remain steadfast because Jesus has not led them to the fiery, intimidating mountain at Sinai; rather, he has led them to the threshold of heaven (Heb. 12:18-23).

Even the Book of Revelation picks up on this latter hope when it recounts a heavenly chorus singing the Song of Moses because the Lord will defeat their enemies (Rev. 15:3). The glorified Christ offers his ear to the tunes of victory just as the Lord did at the shores of the Red Sea. More could be said, but the general point to see is that Moses's role as a deliverer in the Exodus is a key factor in how NT writers understood who Jesus is, what he has done as our Savior, and what it means to follow him as our Lord.

3. Jesus Is the Final Lawgiver

Finally, the NT mentions many similarities between Moses and Jesus because they both gave God's commands to his people. Again, the premiere event where Moses bore this mantle of lawgiver was when he came down from Mount Sinai. He delivered the Ten Commandments as a prelude to the rest of the Law. Then after Israel's horrendous rebellion at Sinai, he later recorded them once more for the nation's future generations. And after the new generation of Israelites was preparing to enter the land of promise under the leadership of Joshua, Moses was responsible for reminding them of the Law and all its expectations one last time.

In a similar fashion, the NT sometimes describes Jesus as a type of lawgiver and uses Mosaic overtones to do it. For instance, two of the times that we read of Jesus being on hills or mountains, the event of Moses delivering the Law seems to be in the background. One example comes in the Sermon on the Mount (Matt 5-7).[37] Here Jesus is offering insights into the kingdom he represents just as Moses gave instruction to Israel on how they were to behave as God's redeemed theocratic nation. He gives credence to the Law when he says that he has come to do something that no one had ever been able to do—keep all of its moral demands, as well as fulfill all of its expectations. Never in this sermon does Jesus appeal to an explicit quotation in the OT and contradict it. Everything Jesus taught was always in harmony with the moral fiber of the Law that Moses delivered to Israel. Yet in this sermon, as well in several other instances, Jesus did criticize things that people "had heard that had been said." When he did, his introductory response was always "but I say unto you."

This insight is intriguing because instead of quoting some rabbi or other Jewish sage as a reputable source to substantiate his claims, Jesus simply asserted his own authority. Jesus thought his claims held their own weight, apart from any other interpretation. He conveyed this same kind of confidence when he would say, "Truly, truly, I say to you." Again, Jesus was basically affirming the dependability of his claims before sharing them. Why? Because he viewed himself as the herald of God's kingdom message to the people. He knew that his words and God's words were inseparable. This is why people would hear his teachings and say they had never heard anyone teach with such "authority." It was because they had never heard the divine lawgiver speak before. It was quite a different experience to hear the Word itself (himself!) speak audibly.

The other mountaintop experience that carries Mosaic overtones was at the aforementioned Transfiguration. After revealing his divine glory to three of his disciples and having an astounding meeting with Moses and Elijah, Jesus returned to the bottom of the mountain to see that his disciples were having trouble performing an exorcism. Just as Moses came down from Mount Sinai with the Ten Commandments only to find Israel committing idolatry and all manner of debauchery, Jesus came down from his own heavenly encounter to be faced with the weak faith and failure of his disciples. As the one with authority, Jesus then cast out the demon and provided instruction for his followers on how to be effective servants when faced with similar ordeals in the future. In both of these events, Jesus provided instruction for his listeners that carried authority simply by virtue of the fact that he was the one who spoke them. In the Sermon on the Mount, his lawgiving authority gripped the hearts of his hearers and after the Mount of Transfiguration, his power as the Son of God cast out a spiritual servant of Satan.

FINAL SALVATION IN JESUS

Along with figures like Abraham, Isaac, Jacob, and King David, Moses no doubt holds a major spot in Israel's hall of fame. He is beloved as the nation's first great prophet, its great deliverer in the Exodus, and the solemn lawgiver who stood between heaven and earth at Mount Sinai. Yet as cherished as he was and as crucial a role that he played in biblical history, his accomplishments were signs that ultimately directed people to a greater prophet, deliverer, and lawgiver who would be the Savior not of Israel from Egypt, but of believing Jews and Gentiles from sin and death.

As impressive as defeating Pharaoh and Egypt with the ten plagues was, making a spectacle of Satan and his demonic hoards by defeating the curse of death was far greater. In Moses's case, his greatness as a leader was only a precursor to the supremacy of the Savior. Thus, John the Gospel writer was right when he said that while Moses gave the Law, God's final saving grace and truth came through Jesus Christ (Jn. 1:17).

DISCUSSION

List a few truths you learned in this chapter that you'd not seen in Scripture before.

How do these truths apply to your life?

Why are these truths important to share with others?

5
ISRAEL

Everyone knows that a hit movie has the potential for a sequel. Follow-up flicks can bring a great story to a close, or they can be a total dud that does not do justice to the original. Whether it be poor acting, disjointed storytelling, or just not retaining the same magic as the previous feature, a poor sequel can spoil a movie goer's enthusiasm. Unfortunately, sequels rarely live up to the hype. More often than not, they dilute the original story, making audiences wish the sequel had never been released.

This section is largely dedicated to showing that storytelling is an important feature of the Bible. As we have discussed in other chapters, the OT begins with an account of the creation of the earth and its first inhabitants, Adam and Eve. The first man was in union with his wife and with the Lord in a bustling garden. And they were delegated with a divine mandate to be stewards over the earth. Indeed, as the Lord himself said, all of this was "very good." But again, shortly into the story, conflict threatens to derail everything. Adam and Eve rebelled against the one single prohibition that the Lord gave them, which brought corruption, conflict, and death upon creation. It even resulted in Adam and Eve being banished from the Lord's presence. Yet like any good story, it does not end in conflict, but rather develops into a thrilling conclusion.

THE HEART OF THE BIBLICAL STORY

Scripture shows two themes that run side-by-side. One is the sobering reality that humanity, as the collective descendants of Adam, live out the tragedies of Eden over and over—except at more extreme levels. Mankind begins with simple disobedience and pride (that is bad enough!), but moves forward to murder and the eventual flooding of the whole earth in an act of judgment.[38] Thankfully, alongside this sad motif, is the parallel truth that God promises to bring salvation to humanity and creation. These two truths are inextricably linked in the biblical story. One describes humanity's problem; the other describes the solution.

We see these two themes beginning to overlap right after Adam's fall, when God announces the curses that are to come upon humanity and the earth. The Lord then turns his attention to the serpent and promises that the seed of a woman will eventually defeat him. He assures Satan that while he will attempt to bruise the heel of this future seed, the seed will ultimately step on him, crushing his head (Gen. 3:15). This is where the story of humanity's sin and God's promises of salvation intersect and even clash. The Lord's promise to heal humanity necessarily entails his equal commitment to defeat Satan. Significant tension occurs in Scripture's story because the sinful inclinations of humanity and the nefarious strategies of Satan constantly fight against the coming of the promised seed that will come to set things right. And a central character that fits into this drama as it unfolds is the nation of Israel.

On the one hand, Israel represents Adam, because like any nation, it was made up of fallen people. On the other hand, Israel was also chosen to channel the blessings of salvation to other nations by being the source of a second Adam, the promised seed of Genesis 3: Jesus Christ. Consequently, the story of Israel is about Adam's failure as well as Christ's victory. It begins at the outset by describing how Israel lived out her early history and developed her hopes for a deliverer. Then it transitions to show how Jesus came to conclude her story, so that both Israel and the nations could receive God's promises. Adam's fall is the first act of Scripture's saga, and the next act features the story of Israel as she awaits her Messiah. The next act, the sequel to the OT, is the coming of Jesus to defeat sin and Satan, fulfilling God's promises to redeem a people.

SETTING THE STAGE FOR ISRAEL'S STORY

Before we can properly understand how Jesus completes Israel's story, and thereby the Bible as a whole, we should first consider where Israel's story begins. One may think that we should start with the nation's inception when God first reached out to Abraham. However, Israel's history is actually an outflow of the story of Adam, encapsulating the same problems and ordeals discussed in the early parts of Genesis. So, if we want to grasp the significance of Israel as well as the role of her Messiah, we must see how they connect with earlier parts of the OT story.

To begin, it should be highlighted that the consequences of Adam's sin emerge repeatedly throughout early stories in the OT. We see interpersonal conflict, relational alienation from the Lord, misconceptions about how to atone for sin, impending death, and finally, being exiled from the place of the Lord's presence. All of these factors are part of the moral decay that had settled into the very fibers of the human race..

For instance, we read that the corruption of Adam entered the hearts of his children. So much so that he his son, Cain, actually became increasingly hostile toward the Lord and his brother Abel, to the point that he became the first recorded murderer. Remember, when the Lord confronted Adam, he blamed both his wife and God. It was Eve who brought him the forbidden fruit, and it was the Lord who brought Eve to him in the first place. But when the Lord later confronted Cain about his actions, he was even more defiant. He brazenly claimed that he was not his brother's keeper. Thus, we see that Adam's shameful irresponsibility had regressed into Cain's violent anger. And as the story progresses, this moral spiral continued to nosedive so much that the Lord was forced to take serious measures.

1. Noah and the Flood

The most climactic example of this comes in the story of Noah. Following the development of early civilizations, which again had their original roots in Adam, wickedness continually escalated across the earth. Added to humanity's growing depravity was also a bizarre event that occurred between the Sons of God and the daughters of men, which tested the limits of the Lord's patience (Gen. 6:1-4).[39] He then lamented that humanity was hopelessly evil and thereby promised to send a flood. He was, in a sense, going to give the earth a bath by judging all the descendants of Adam, that is except for one faithful remnant: Noah and his family. This was a critical moment in early biblical history, because humanity had reached such a depraved low. As opposed to one couple being kicked out of a garden, sin had become so widespread that almost every inhabitant on the earth was under judgment.

However, even though this judgment and cleansing was deserved, such an act would obviously threaten God's earlier promise to produce a seed that would crush the serpent. It would be impossible to keep such a promise if humanity was completely wiped out. This is why the preservation of Noah was so important. Even amidst all the debauchery of humanity, the Lord still preserved a remnant because a flood was not to be the end of the story. A seed of a woman that would redeem humanity and crush the serpent was to have the last word. God would make good on his promise.

2. The Tower of Babel

After the flood and subsequent repopulation of the earth by Noah's descendants, the developing nations showed that they still retained Adam's fallenness. We see this in an account where Genesis tells us that that many wanted to remain unified in one location and avoid possible dispersion. So, they chose to build a tower that could reach to the heavens (Gen. 11:1-9). This act was filled with irony because now instead of wanting to be like God by knowing good from evil, the nations wanted to invade God's heavenly territory and exalt their own renown. Furthermore, by trying to escape the earth and make their way to heaven, they are reversing God's blueprint for redeeming creation and once again dwelling with mankind.[40] Had they succeeded, Revelation 21-22 would be a fairytale, not a promise.

Eventually the Lord then came down to inspect their attempts. They said, "Come let us make bricks…" and, "Come let us build…," but God declared, "Come let us confuse their language…"[41] The paradox here is that the nations' stated motive for building this tower was to avoid being divided. However, the very thing that still unified them was taken away, namely their commonly used language. The result of this judgment was a more excessive version of Eden because while Adam and Eve left the garden, they did it together. In this judgment, the nations were scattered across the earth being alienated from each other.

Yet at the same time, we must remember that when these tragedies occurred, every expression of divine judgment included related promises of salvation. God was not going to abandon humanity altogether, although sometimes things did look bleak. Yes, Adam and Eve were banished—nevertheless, they were assured that the serpent was still doomed. The tower of Babel indeed resulted in disaster because the nations were divided and scattered. But this dispersion of the nations actually set the stage for the Lord's choice of a man who would the progenitor of a nation that would bring blessings to all others. In both of these cases, then, we see that God's acts of judgment against sin are placed alongside his related promises to preserve a remnant who will receive salvation. There will be a "humanity" who will see the serpent defeated and a nation composed of all nations that will receive salvific favor.[42]

So even though humanity was no longer in Eden, the long process of defeating Satan was still in motion. The early preservation of believers in the ancient world, as well as the promise to Noah that a flood would not destroy the world, were signs of this. Adam's story was not to end in defeat. Following the failure of Babel, the biblical narrative takes an important turn by introducing a new wrinkle. We begin to learn about the life of a man and a people who the Lord would use to produce the promised redeemer, the long-awaited seed of a woman—and this is where Israel comes on the scene.

THE BIRTH OF ISRAEL

It is easy to see in the early chapters of Genesis that people who lived before and immediately after the flood still replicated Adam's faults. We discussed this in more detail in a previous chapter. Suffice it to say, none of these early generations fell far from the tree. Adam's story still remained in dire need of resolution. That is why the flood was sent to judge the earth and why the descendants of Noah, who produced all the subsequent nations, were scattered at the tower of Babel. Mankind was still riddled with sin, needing healing and restoration. God was well aware of this dilemma, but was not confused or defeated. That is why he preserved Noah's family and scattered the nations at Babel instead of annihilating them. Those who speak of "the God of the OT" and his maniacal anger issues have clearly never read the OT closely. What he says of himself turns out to be true:

> *"The Lord—the Lord is a compassionate and gracious God,*
> *slow to anger and abounding in faithful love and truth,*
> *maintaining faithful love to a thousand generations, forgiving*
> *iniquity, rebellion, and sin. But he will not leave the guilty*
> *unpunished, bringing the fathers' iniquity on the children and*
> *grandchildren to the third and fourth generation."* (Ex. 34:6-7)

Now the story of Genesis progresses to show how the Lord would produce his world-saving seed. We discover that he would accomplish this goal by creating a new nation that could serve as a funnel through which divine blessings could be poured out to all others. This meant that Adam and Even's failure to cover the earth with divine image-bearers would be remedied by a nation that would become a beacon of hope for all the nations. And this chosen people was birthed through God's choice of one man, Abram, whose name was later changed to Abraham (cf., Gen. 12:1, 17:5).

1. The Father of Israel: The Role of Abraham

We read in Genesis that after the fiasco in Babel, God chose to show his favor on Abram, a man from the land of Ur of the Chaldeans, who at the time was living in Haran. He commanded him to take his family and leave his relatives and homeland (cf., Gen. 12:1a; Acts 7:2-4). Abram was assured that if he embarked on this pilgrimage, he would be given a land and become the source of a great nation, which would bring blessings to other nations (Gen. 12:1b-2). Later, these promises were confirmed in a covenant that was sealed with a ritual of sacrifice (Gen. 15:7-17). Here the Lord added the promise that Abraham would have a son through whom his descendants would multiply to an innumerable degree (Gen. 15:1-6). Abraham was also reminded that his line would eventually inherit a promised area of land some four generations in the future (Gen. 15:18-19). Furthermore, this covenant was marked by a custom of remembrance via the practice of circumcision, because the promise of blessing started with Abraham's offspring (Gen. 17).

Abraham clearly was to be a central figure in God's plan. Adam's story was now receiving a new chapter because divine blessings were going to be bestowed on one of his descendants, in a specified land, with a family of offspring. What still remained to be seen was how God would fulfill these promises and whether Abraham's descendants would have the same kind of faith that he had in his walk with the Lord. Despite his listed failures, Abraham was a man of faith who later was called a "a friend of God" (cf., Isa. 41:8; Jms. 2:23). The question on the table was whether the promised descendants of this future nation would choose to embrace that identity or not. Would they allow themselves to be used by the Lord to add a new chapter to Adam's and now Abraham's story? Would they be faithful to their faithful God?

2. The Father of the Israelites: The Role of Jacob

Jacob's role became a factor in Israel's story even before he was born. Abraham's son, Isaac, who was the miracle child through whom the promised nation would come, had married a young cousin named Rebekah. They were having difficulty conceiving when the Lord intervened and she became pregnant with twin boys who came to be named Esau and Jacob. The Lord later told Rebekah that these boys represented two major nations, and that the older son would be subordinate to, or serve, the younger. This prediction foreshadowed future tensions between Esau and Jacob. When they became adults, Jacob exploited Esau's shortsighted brashness by duping him into surrendering his birthright for a bite to eat. Then after this encounter put a wedge between them, Jacob took further measures by tricking his ailing father into giving him the paternal blessing that belonged to Esau as the firstborn. Now, when Esau found out what happened, his contempt for his brother reached the boiling point. He was going to bide his time until his father died and then, in the footsteps of Cain, he would kill his brother. Rebekah found out about this scheme and warned Jacob about Esau's plans.

After receiving further instruction from Isaac, Jacob fled his home and went north to Paddan-aram in the land of Haran, where his uncle Laban lived. During this journey, the story reveals an important twist because it was here that he had a dream. Jacob saw a ladder or heavenly staircase, with angels traversing on it and heard the Lord speak from its tip. Jacob was assured that he was to be the next link in the chain of recipients for the Abrahamic promises (Gen. 28:10-17). The next morning, Jacob named this area Bethel ("house of God" or "God's dwelling place") and continued on his way to Laban's home. And it was here where Jacob's previous antics backfired on him.

Upon arriving at Laban's, Jacob fell in love with Laban's younger daughter, Rachel. But before he could marry her, the trickster was himself deceived by Laban into first marrying her older sister, Leah. After arguing with Laban about this fiasco and later marrying Rachel, Jacob became involved in constant drama. He was in ongoing deliberations with Laban, his employer and new father-in-law. He also lived with the stress of having two wives who were sisters. Hopefully we will never know what this feels like, but we can imagine the drama. Beyond the typical sibling rivalry nightmare, they were also at odds with each other because early on Rachel could not conceive. However, all of this stress did subside with Jacob having twelve boys from both Rachel and Leah as well as their two maidservants, Bilhah and Zilpah (Gen. 29:31-30:24). These sons became the seedbed for the future twelve tribes of Israel.

Several years later, Jacob's difficulties with Laban came to a head and he was advised to travel south to his homeland. Now while in transit in the region of Gilead, Laban and his sons caught up with him and things looked bleak. Fortunately, the Lord intervened and they made a pact to resolve their issues. But the impending reality that Jacob still had to face was his brother Esau. Shortly after Laban returned home, Jacob encountered some angelic messengers who encouraged him. But he still remained reticent about meeting Esau. Who could blame him? He surmised that it might be prudent to send messengers to greet him with blessings and gifts. When they left, they apparently met Esau's company because they relayed a message back to Jacob that Esau was coming to meet with a large company. Jacob understandably became fearful of potential vengeance and began dividing his camp up into segments so that they would approach Esau in waves. Hopefully if Esau received the first groups in peace, it would be a sign that Jacob and his family would be safe. Even so, on the night before meeting his brother, Jacob crossed the river in Jabbok presumably to pray in solitude.

This is where we are then told that Jacob encountered a "man" with whom he wrestled all night until daybreak (Gen. 32:24). Their struggle reached its climax when the "man" (Jacob identifies him as the Lord in human form) supernaturally weakened Jacob to stall their battle. However, this did not weaken Jacob's resolve because he refused to let go until he was blessed. This is a critical moment because for one, Jacob had already been blessed bountifully while living in Laban's household. Also, God had already told him that he was the next heir in the Abrahamic line. Here, though, Jacob wanted his own blessing in this story. The challenge: he had to fool the Lord himself. Of course, all he could do was humbly beg. The Lord said his name would no longer be Jacob ("trickster"); rather it would now be Israel, the "one who strives after the Lord" or "a prince of God."

The next morning, the newly invigorated Jacob was able to meet his brother, Esau. And when he did, they both put their past behind them. They welcomed each other in a compassionate embrace and eventually parted ways, Esau going back to the land of Seir (or Edom) and Jacob going west back into Canaan where he traversed through Shechem, Bethel, and finally Hebron. Then we discover that years later, Jacob's family made their way to the land of Egypt because of providential dealings in the life of his son, Joseph (Gen. 37-47). And this would set the stage for future generations to experience God's deliverance in the Exodus event.

THE STORY OF ISRAEL AS A NATION

We see up to this point how Israel's identity was carefully put into place. Each of its Patriarchs were directly chosen and even named by the Lord. He changed Abram's name to reflect the divine promise that he would father many nations. Isaac's name was given by the Lord to be a constant reminder that Abraham's wife, Sarah, laughed when it was promised that she would have a son in her old age. And again, Jacob's name was changed because he received a special blessing from the Lord at Jabbok. All of these men received new identities because they were chosen during the embryonic stage of a nation, which in time would bring new blessings to Adam's progeny. Now with all of these divine road markers in place, it was time for subsequent generations to move the story forward. Do not worry, dear reader: Jesus will be on the scene eventually.

Abraham, Isaac, and Jacob are now off the scene. The term "Israel" is no longer being used just as the name of the Hebrew people's forefather anymore—it's taking on the broader connotation of the "sons of Israel." In other words, Israel is no longer a person, but a people. And as this part of their history unfolds, several common features of Israel's identity rise to the surface. In fact, they are at the forefront of Israel's existence when Jesus arrives on the scene centuries later.

1. Israel as God's People

The main event that solidifies Israel as a people and nation is the Exodus. Here, Israel became enslaved to the Egyptian powers. But in his perfect timing, God intervenes by sending Moses to guide them to the Abrahamic land of promise. When the Lord summons Moses for this task at the burning bush, he identifies himself as the God of Abraham, Isaac, and Jacob. He then proceeds to refer to the Hebrews as "his people." Moses and his brother Aaron echo this claim later when they face the Pharaoh to tell him that the Lord demands "his people" be set free. This language is by no means arbitrary. It is grounded in the promises that the Lord has already made to the Patriarchs. The people belong to the Lord because the only reason they exist is on account of his prior activity with their forefathers. It is also why the Lord later ratifies a Mosaic covenant with Israel in terms that bond him to the people. He claims that "I will be their God and they will be my people" (e.g., Ex 6:6-7; 19:5; Lev 26:9-14). This means they are a special possession to him, elected heirs of specific blessings and bearers of significant responsibilities.

Additionally, this language of inheritance becomes the basis for other OT metaphors that the Lord uses to describe Israel such as a son, wife, and vineyard. Israel belongs to the Lord in a similar way that a son does to a father, a wife to a husband, or a vineyard to a creator. It is unique, intimate, and even familial. God is giving indications to his people that they are not only his creations or his subjects—they are his family. This will become clearer when Jesus enters the story.

2. Israel as a Covenant Benefactor

A second feature, which goes hand in hand with the previous concept, is that the nation is a special recipient of divine promises. As the Lord's people, they are in a covenant agreement with him. We have already seen this in the choosing of Abraham and his descendants through Isaac and Jacob. They are to receive the promises of a land and place of prominence. This is also why the Lord delivers them out of Egypt, so that those promises can finally begin to reach fulfillment.

Yet after the Exodus event, during their travels through Sinai to Canaan, the Lord establishes another agreement with Israel. Its legal parameters serve as a kind of constitution that the people are to follow as God's chosen "nation." They received this covenant when they reached Mount Sinai. They had a ceremonial gathering with Moses serving as their mediator. Moses met with the Lord atop Mount Sinai and received the Law, a specific code for living. Under the Lord's instruction, Moses documented its demands, which contained legal, economic, social, personal, and liturgical guidelines that the people were to follow. By doing so, they would function as priestly representatives and set-apart citizens of a newly established kingdom of which the Lord was king (Ex. 19:6). Moreover, this covenant promised blessings if it was followed, and curses if it was violated (Ex. 20:1-21; Lev. 26; Deut. 4:26-27, 36-38; 5:2-5).

Unlike the Abrahamic covenant, the Mosaic agreement included stipulations in which Israel's experience of the Abrahamic blessings were contingent upon their obedience. Put another way, the experience of Abrahamic blessing for each particular generation of Israelites (and the individuals within Israel) was dependent upon covenant faithfulness to the Mosaic covenant. It is crucial to keep in mind that the Law also became part of the backdrop for how God would later establish a king over Israel. Furthermore, when more covenants were promised to Israel such as the Davidic or new covenant, they were still all tied in various ways to the previous treaties made through Abraham and Moses. What we discover is that God's earlier promise to address Adam's failure becomes inseparable from these other developing layers of promises that God makes with Israel. It was to be through Israel, who is blessed, that other nations could be blessed.

3. Israel as a Kingdom-Nation

A third component, which in some ways is the most important, is that Israel comes to be identified as a kingdom ruled by the Lord and/or his chosen ruler. This nationalistic quality emerges especially after Israel receives the Mosaic covenant and later enters the Promised Land under the leadership of Joshua. It then becomes a full-blown issue in Israel's history once the nation becomes a monarchy. The period of Israelite kings was jumpstarted when the people expressed a desire to have a king (rather than judges) because they wanted to be like their surrounding nations. Their first choice was a man named Saul, which ended in disaster. During this debacle, the Lord selected David, though he did not become king for some time after Saul's death (2 Sam. 5:1-4). When he became king, however, he galvanized the morale of the people. And in time, he also expressed a desire to build a temple in which the Ark of the Covenant could rest (2 Sam. 7:1-3). This elicited a response from the Lord who, through the prophet Nathan, informed him that he would build David a house, which entailed the declaration of a new promissory covenant (cf., 2 Sam. 7:12-16; 1 Chron. 17:11-14).

The agreement was that David's lineage would become a dynasty and produce a ruler who would extend the Abrahamic blessings to Israel, as well as other nations who would submit to this royal seed. In the end, then, this covenant narrowed the focus of the Abrahamic promises because the seed was now Davidic (cf., Gen. 3:15; 18:18; 22:18; 26:4; 28:14; 35:11; 38:49; 49:10; Ruth 4:18-22). A descendant of both Abraham and David would be a king who would reign on a throne over an Israel-centric kingdom in the land of promise. Simple enough, right? What this did is establish an irreversible political element to Israel's story. Their role was not merely couched in terms of God working through them to provide blessings; it was now defined in terms of God working through their kings to rule over them and ultimately the world.

4. Israel as a Covenant Breaker

The fourth and final factor that permeates Israel's story is the consistent violation of their covenantal obligations. Even though they were bestowed with the Abrahamic, Mosaic, and Davidic mantles, they still carried the DNA of Jacob's deceitfulness, Cain's treachery, and ultimately Adam's fallenness. For example, we see Israel committing egregious idolatry before the Mosaic covenant was even fully ratified. Then after they received forgiveness, they reached the southern border of the Promised Land only to refuse to enter because of their unbelief. This failure resulted in the death of the majority of those who saw God's greatness in the Exodus. And when the next generation entered Canaan under Joshua's leadership, they still failed to eliminate all of the false religions in the land.

These competing religions resulted in Israel's constant idolatry and rebellion in the book of Judges. And later, when Israel entered the period of the monarchy, Saul proved to be a spiritual train wreck, David orchestrated a horrendous cover-up because he committed adultery and murder, and Solomon allowed pagan idolatry to spread throughout the land, which ultimately ended in the splitting of the kingdom when his son Rehoboam took over as king.

Added to this, both divisions of Israel (the Northern and Southern kingdoms) later went into exile for their unrepentant sinfulness. And even when Israelites were allowed to return to Canaan decades later, the prophet Malachi railed against them for committing many of the same sins that their parents did. In a sense, the story of Israel was replicating the ancient wrestling match between Jacob and the Lord.[43] The only difference was that, here, the way to be blessed was to obey, not simply ask for it. So, a huge question mark had been placed at this point of Israel's history. Could anyone use his/her life to tell a story where Adam or Israel obeys the Lord? Could anyone be an obedient servant who could qualify as a vicarious representative for those who were disobedient? This is where the promised seed of Genesis 3, the one who could crush the serpent and complete Israel's mission, finally steps on the scene.

JESUS AS THE FULFILLMENT OF ISRAEL'S STORY

Jesus came on the historical scene when Israel's anticipation to see God keep his covenantal promises was at an all-time high. And rightfully so. The Jewish people were awaiting a leader who would defeat their enemies, reestablish their sovereignty in the land of promise, liberate them from foreign powers, and solidify the nation's identity. Israel wanted this figure, or Messiah, to grant their divine sanctions so their shortcomings could be forgotten and, ultimately, Adam's failure rectified. Basically, Israel was waiting for opening night of the final sequel to their hopes when creation would once again be at peace. However, Jesus would introduce several unexpected chapters to Israel's story, catching many people by surprise.

Israel's hopes were going to be fulfilled. But all of their expectations were going to be centered on Jesus himself. He was going to reconfigure Israel's expectations in such a way that he became the cipher for decoding their true significance. Not only that, he was also going to relive Israel's story. His life was going to retell it in such a way that Israel, through a true Israelite, would obey God and be faithful to all of their covenantal obligations. Jesus was going to embody Israel's life through his own, and by doing so, Israel would finally have a prototype of a faithful Jew to be their representative. This is why the NT presents Jesus as the true Israel who replicates, fulfills, and completes the nation's story. He was what Israel needed to be--covenant-keeping and victorious. Likewise, he would provide atonement for sin so that the curse of death could be lifted and the serpent could finally begin to receive the final blows of defeat. All in all, Jesus was going to be the perfect sequel to the entire biblical narrative.

And the best way to see how Jesus accomplished this feat is by observing two simple ways in which NT portrays Jesus in relationship to Israel.

1. Jesus, the Son of Man Who Institutes a new covenant

The first important feature is Jesus's teaching on the nature of the kingdom that Israel was waiting for. Here, Jesus clearly emphasized that its point of origin was heaven, not Jerusalem. This was quite a jolt to many of his original hearers, because most of them justifiably viewed God's coming rule in terms of the earthly promises made to Abraham, Moses, and David. The kingdom was supposed to be located in the land of Canaan (Abrahamic), with the blessing of protection when obedience to the Law was upheld (Mosaic), and under the leadership of the right descendant (Davidic). Now according to Jesus, none of these factors were untrue at face value. This is why, for example, the Gospels provide genealogies showing that Jesus was a part of the Davidic line; that he had come to fulfill the Law; and that his followers would inherit the earth/land. But along with these points, Jesus claimed that Israel's earthly kingdom could only be what it should be if someone from heaven established it. In short, Israel and the world needed a New Jerusalem.

This is one reason why Jesus often referred to himself as the "Son of Man." This title derives from a prophetic vision in Daniel 7:11-14, where an agent from heaven is delegated by the Lord ("the Ancient of Days"), to exercise authority over all the nations of the earth. Jesus attested to this role, claiming that his kingdom was the one that Israel was eagerly awaiting. Yet again, their kingdom was coming from heaven, not Mount Zion. This is why, for instance, when the Roman leader Pontius Pilate interrogated Jesus, he did not deny being the King of the Jews. Rather, he simply emphasized that the nature of his kingship and the kingdom he represented was not of this world (Jn. 18:33-36).

We see this point made on an earlier occasion where Jesus combined this Son of Man idea with Jacob's vision of the heavenly ladder. He told his disciple Nathanael that he would one day see heaven opened with the angels ascending and descending on the Son of Man (Jn. 1:51). In other words, Jacob's vision of a staircase to heaven would now be the highway that Jesus would use to bring heaven's reign to earth.[44] The Gospels show, then, that someone who was uniquely related to the heavenly Father, not just David, could only fulfill Israel's earthly hopes. And only Jesus fit the criteria.

Likewise, on the other side of this coin, Jesus as the heavenly Son of Man was arriving to ratify a new covenant (NC). The original background to the promise of a NC pertained to the barrage of curses endured by Israel because of her consistent unfaithfulness to the Mosaic agreement. It had become crystal clear that the expectations of the Abrahamic and Davidic covenants were being hamstrung by the long list of Mosaic violations. Thus, a dilemma was in need of resolution. The Law, as good and righteous as it was, could not enact the Mosaic blessings because Israel never fully fostered a heart for the God of the Law. This is why the Lord eventually promised that he would establish a final covenant with his people wherein his law would be written on their hearts. They would be forgiven of their sins, inherit eternal life, and be resurrected from the dead both nationally as well as bodily. They also would be restored to their land, never fall into the hands of any enemies, and be protected by a kingly leader with integrity (cf., Jer. 31:33-34; Ezek. 11:19-20; 36:25-27; 37:1-23; Dan. 12:1-2).

For Jesus to speak of the NC was nothing "new" in and of itself. But to couch it in terms that would require Israel's Messiah to die a shameful death to atone for sin was baffling. Just as shocking was the fact that the NC's initial sign of success was not the immediate trouncing of Israel's political enemies or even the immediate recapture of the Promised Land. Rather, it was that Jews (and Gentiles) could be reconciled to God and become part of Christ's heavenly kingdom. This caused quite a stir among many Jews because Jesus came to deliver Israel from itself, Rome. The people needed the new heart promised in the NC so that the curse of judgment, including exile, would no longer be a factor. Destroying Caesar was not the solution—changing Israel's sinful heart was. So, part of the threshold that Israel needed to cross to experience her final chapter of salvation and an eternal kingdom was recognizing that Christ had come from heaven to change her from the inside out. Every Israelite needed to be born again (Jn. 3:7). Going back to the language of family mentioned earlier in the chapter, Israel and all of mankind could be born into a new family through adoption in Christ (Eph. 1:5; cf. Rom. 8:15).

2. Jesus Provides the Final Act in Israel's Script

The other major factor that bound Jesus to Israel was the fact that he identified with the people in their own context, not just as an outside party. He, who shared the heavenly glory of the Father as the eternal son, chose to become incarnate. He was born an "Israelite," even a Nazarene, under the Law so he could provide a fitting sequel to Israel's story (Gal 4:4). Jesus was going to show that the biblical narrative, which began with Adam and now enveloped the people of Israel, was going to end in triumph, not tragic defeat. The striving and waiting was about to end.

We see this link between Israel and Jesus early on, for example, when Matthew describes the life of Jesus in terms that coincide with the early life of Israel (God's son) in the Exodus. He begins by describing Jesus as an innocent infant who was providentially protected as Moses was and later came out of Egypt just as Israel did (Matt. 2:15). Then as an adult, just as Israel became bound to Moses in their deliverance at the Red Sea, Jesus embraced solidarity with Israel by receiving the baptism of repentance that John the Baptizer was proclaiming at the Jordan (Matt. 3:13-17). After performing this act, he departed from the water so he could show himself to be the one who would faithfully endure testing in the wilderness (Matt. 4:11). After exemplifying himself as the ideal Israelite, Jesus preaches the Sermon on the Mount, an overview of the laws of his kingdom, just as Moses originally gave the Law to Israel at Mount Sinai (Matt. 5:1-2).

Likewise, the apostle John in his Gospel highlights similar parallels between Israel's early experiences as a nation and Jesus's identity as the Messiah. John highlights instances where Jesus claimed that he is the new bread from heaven (as opposed to manna) and the water of life (as opposed to the water from a rock), which only requires one to drink of it once (cf., Jn. 4:14; 6:41; 1 Cor. 10:1-4). The point of these connections is that while God provided for Israel in the Exodus, Jesus now claims to encapsulate all of these provisions as Israel's redeemer.

Along these lines, Jesus goes even further than just re-enacting parts of Israel's old script. He also restricts the definition of what it means to be part of the true Israel. Most notably, he teaches that only those who believe in him and follow him as his disciples can remain in the biblical story. Jesus, then, determines who can be part of the active cast of Israel's sequel. Only those who embrace him as the Messiah can be part of God's people, inherit the new creation, and be delivered from Satan and death.

This point is fleshed out in numerous ways throughout the NT. For example, major OT images that are used to illustrate Israel's covenantal relationship with the Lord are sometimes ascribed to Jesus and his role as the world's savior such as a vine or a flock of sheep. He claims that he is the vine to which one must be connected, and only those who hear his voice are part of God's flock (Jn. 10:11-16; 15:1-5). Jesus even goes so far as to call twelve disciples (parallel to the tribes of Jacob-Israel) and promises them (excluding Judas Iscariot, of course) that they will one day be rulers over Israel (Matt. 19:28). What is even more interesting is that they are listed on the foundations of the heavenly Jerusalem that comes out of heaven to the earth in John apocalyptic vision, as well (Rev. 21:14).

Furthermore, on numerous occasions Jesus got into hot water with the Jewish leaders of his day when he interpreted definitive markers of Jewish identity in light of his role as the Messiah. For example, the meticulous details of Sabbath-keeping, as decreed by Jewish traditions, were scrutinized because Jesus claimed to be the Lord of the Sabbath, even greater than the Sabbath (cf., Matt. 12:8; Lk 6:1-11). Another significant revision pertained to the sacred Passover. Now instead of celebrating Israel's exodus from Egypt, Jesus proposed a revised version of it that pointed to the upcoming deliverance from sin through the NC (see Matt. 26:26-29; Lk. 22:14-20).

And finally, Jesus showed that the need for continual Levitical sacrifices was nullified because of his once-for-all death for the sins of the world (cf., Jn. 1:29; Heb. 9:28; 1 Pet. 3:8). The Levitical priesthood was to be put out of business because the clean/unclean dilemma, as well as the ongoing need for atonement, was nullified. Henceforth, there would be no need for a temple because Jesus provided full access to the Father via his new priestly office (Heb. 7:23-24). In essence, then, the Mosaic framework that fostered a distinct religious identity for Israel was being phased out because their story was transitioning to NC terms in light of Christ's redemptive work. Israel was now under new management because of who Jesus was and what he had accomplished.

FULFILLING ISRAEL'S STORY

In every area where Israel failed, Jesus succeeded. And the implications of such a fact meant that various features of Israel's story were now being rectified, expanded, and clarified. The reason being that the entire storyline of the nation was now being enveloped by Jesus who, though being a part of Israel's line and David's family, was no descendent of Adam. Therefore, the final sequel of Israel's (and Adam's) story had been written, and ended with a triumph. This is good news for us, because without the Son of God who became the Son of Man, we could not be sons and daughters of God. And without a grand finale to Israel's story, we would have no part in the bigger story.

DISCUSSION

List a few truths you learned in this chapter that you'd not seen in Scripture before.

How do these truths apply to your life?

Why are these truths important to share with others?

6
DAVIDIC KINGS

We are all familiar with the slogan, "Power corrupts and absolute power corrupts absolutely." If history has taught us anything, it is that people are prone to abuse authority. Looking to safeguard against potential dictators, we cry out for governmental structures with "checks and balances," hoping to curb corruption.

At face value, checks and balances are helpful. We should hold onto anything that might keep dishonest authority at bay. But the problem is, Scripture teaches the reason power intoxicates people's egos is because they are already corrupt, whether they have any power or not. Power simply exposes the inherent corruption of the human heart.

But what if there could be a leader or ruler who was not held back by the shortcomings of greed, lust, or ego? This might sound crazy, but what if a king existed who was just, righteous, and powerful while at the same time compassionate, merciful, and gracious? This would seem almost too good to be true. But it is one of the most important concerns in the Bible.

The narrative of Scripture begins with creation that is governed by God and his delegated servants, Adam and Eve. As we saw in Chapter 1, after they chose to trade their authority as his vice-regents for Satan's lie, there was now no incorrupt ruler on the earth. However, God declared that he would defeat Satan and his deceptive antics with the seed of the woman (Gen. 3:15). Just as Satan tried to usurp God's authority and corrupt humanity, the Lord declared war against him by promising that there would be one to come who would serve as humanity's representative and deliverer.

Creation would not remain kingless. This was an immense promise for God to make—so big that it takes the rest of the Bible to unveil how he would keep it. And when the perfect, righteous king finally comes, it will be worth the wait.

THE BACKDROP FOR THE PERFECT KING

The Bible begins the Perfect King's story by focusing on the solemn promises of the Lord throughout OT history. We refer to these oaths as covenants, which are official agreements that God makes with various individuals and/or groups. They included the granting of certain privileges, blessings, and responsibilities as well as possible means of punishment and discipline if the involved parties deviated from their part of the agreement(s). Two important covenants set the stage for where we are going in this chapter.

First, God made a covenant with Abram, whose name was later changed to Abraham (Gen. 12:1, 17:5). This served as the foundation on which God's restored rule would come to the earth; namely through one man who would father one nation, which ultimately would unite all others. God told Abram (later Abraham) to take his family and leave everything, including his relatives and homeland (Gen. 12:1; Acts 7:2-4). The Lord promised Abram that if he would respond in faith, he would be given a land and become a predecessor of a great nation that would bring blessings to other nations (Gen. 12:1-2, 15:1-19). God kept this promise, and Abraham's descendants became the seedbed for the twelve tribes of Israel (Gen. 29:31-30:24, 32:28).

The second major covenant is with Moses. Through the Exodus, the Lord showed his superiority over all of Egypt's gods and laid claim to Israel as his people. Their freedom from slavery served as a national moment of liberation. The God of Abraham kept his promise and laid claim to his people (Ex. 6:6-7, 19:5). This was no cakewalk, though. Israel would have to relate to God on new terms as a nation under a new constitution.

At Mount Sinai, Moses was appointed as the mediator between the people and the Lord. Moses was given the Law, and his people were constituted as priestly representatives and set-apart citizens of a newly established kingdom ruled by the Lord (Ex. 19:6). The covenant entailed blessings if it was followed, and curses if it was violated (Ex. 20:1-21; Lev. 26; Deut. 4:26-38, 5:2-5). These demands applied to the people as well as any potential rulers of Israel. The Law, then, became part of the backdrop for how God would later establish a king over Israel.

FROM DAVID TO HIS DESCENDANTS

At the latter part of Samuel's ministry as judge over Israel, the people requested a king because they desired to be like the surrounding nations (1 Sam. 8:4-5). God knew that this request was wrongly motivated by their dissatisfaction with his divine kingship. This is why he warned them of the dangers of this request (1 Sam. 8:10-18). Still, they were adamant, so Saul was named the first King of Israel. Though his rule began with promise, Saul disobeyed the Lord's instructions and the kingdom was taken away from him (1 Sam. 13:8-23, 15:1-23). God wanted a king whose heart was devoted to him. Insert: David.

David was initially anointed by Samuel when he was still young and shepherding his family's flocks (1 Sam. 26), yet he would not be fully inaugurated for fifteen years or so, after Saul died and the nation agreed that he was the rightful choice (2 Sam. 5:1-4). He proceeded to galvanize the nation's morale by bringing the Ark of the Covenant back to Jerusalem (2 Sam. 6:12-23). Then after the pomp and circumstance of this triumphant event, David began to express concern that the Lord's manifest presence in the Ark was located in a tent, while he himself lived in luxurious house of cedar (2 Sam. 7:1-3).

The Lord responded to David's honorable intentions by telling the prophet Nathan to inform him that he would build David a house (2 Sam. 7:12-16; 1 Chron. 17:11-14). This promise was the Lord's commitment to preserve David's lineage, thereby building a dynasty which would inherit the promises of the Abrahamic covenant and ensure that those who followed this royal seed would receive them as well. This promise would be fulfilled through a divine act of adopting David's male descendants. This is why the Lord's pledge began with the declaration that Solomon would build the Temple, and then stated that the Davidic line would be adopted as God's sons (2 Sam. 7:13-14). Yet like Israel as God's son by covenant (Ex 4:22-23), David's regal posterity as God's son by covenant also entailed the possibility of divine discipline if a king fell into disobedience.[45] Still the Lord would not take the kingdom away from David's family as he did with Saul (2 Sam. 7:14-15; 1 Chron. 17:13). He had a promise to keep.

In the end, this covenant narrowed the focus of the Abrahamic promises because the seed was now identified to be specifically Davidic (Gen 3:15, 22:18, 35:11, 38:49, 49:10; Ruth 4:18-22). The king, a descendant of both Abraham and David, would reign on a throne over an Israel-centric kingdom in the land of promise. And the overflow of this reign would bring blessings to all other nations.

The Davidic king would be held to a high standard. God did not want another Saul. He put checks and balances in place for his nation's leader. But this was not some American three-branch system of elected delegates. Divine Law would be the check and the balance.

GOD'S LAW: THE CHECK AND THE BALANCE

Long before this Davidic covenant was revealed, the Mosaic economy actually anticipated an eventual transition from a strict theocracy to a monarchy. We see this in God's prediction that the people would want a king to be like the other nations (Deut. 17:14). This showed that God was not blindsided by his people's self-sabotage.

After Israel reached the monumental moment of entering the Promised Land for the first time in 40 years (Num. 13-14; Deut. 2:14), the new generation of Israelites was being reminded of the Law. This led to the composition of Deuteronomy. As they entered Canaan, part of this recounting of the Law entailed specific instructions in Deuteronomy 17:15-20 for the conduct of a future king.[46]

1. A King Must Be a Native Israelite (Deut. 17:15)

The first requirement that Moses mentions is that a future king must be one that the Lord endorses. He cannot simply be a popular choice exclusively determined by a random poll of the people. No fancy signs, smear campaigns, or electoral votes. Like us today, people are prone to look only at the outward appearance and external talents of candidates as opposed to their hearts and inward character. But only God can see such things (1 Sam. 16:7).

Likewise, a potential king must be an Israelite, not a foreigner. Though not mentioned here in Deuteronomy 17, there were at least two motives behind such a restriction. First, Jacob (Israel) himself had already alluded to it. He said that his son, Judah, would forge a tribe within the nation, which would bring forth royalty and rulership (Gen. 49:10-12). Thus, only a son of Israel from this particular clan could potentially fill this role. The other motive for limiting candidates to Israelites is that a foreigner most likely would serve other deities, inevitably trying to merge their pagan ideologies with the kingdom of Israel. Talk about disaster.

2. A King Must Not Multiply Horses (Deut. 17:16)

The first requirement for Israel's potential king is reasonable enough, but the rest of the restrictions seem to be explicitly counter-intuitive. Humanly speaking, they seemingly eliminate all of the necessary strategies for an ancient new covenant king. This command is a perfect example.

A king was not to increase his stables with horses, nor was he to obtain any from Egypt. This was especially tempting for Israel. Egypt was breeding modern-day Triple Crown winners. But simply put, Israel was to consider Egypt as a part of their past, never their present.

This rule is particularly sticky for the Israelite king because horses were part of the military lifeblood of any ancient nation. It was not that any king of Israel would want a large number of horses so they could have entertaining races or enjoyable polo matches. Rather, horses were the elite form of mobility for combat. Soldiers rode them, chariots were pulled by them, and large waves of horses could easily flank and plow over infantry who were on foot. The more horses a king had, the more firepower he could wield against his enemies. Yet Israel's king was forbidden to amass one of the most valuable commodities in ancient warfare because in the end, the Lord was Israel's mightiest warrior (2 Chron. 32:8; Ps. 20:7, 33:17).

3. A King Must Not Have Multiple Wives (Deut. 17:17a)

This restriction gives the impression that the Lord wanted a king to be an upstanding husband in a monogamous relationship. Undoubtedly, a leader was to emulate God's faithfulness to his people by being wholly devoted to one spouse. But something more is going on here.

One way that kings could avoid potential wars and even better, possibly make allies with other nations, was to marry daughters of other monarchs. By marrying into numerous families, kings would solidify alliances and ask for aid from the kingdoms with whom they had made marital ties. While there were unquestionable conjugal advantages that kings would exploit, the other underlying motive for this trend was to build an international military network.

God knew that such antics would lead to disaster because every wife of a pagan nation would normally be committed to a pagan deity of some sort. And if these women were loyal to their national heritages, they would undoubtedly try to persuade their husbands to embrace their religions. Moreover, if a king had multiple wives from various nations, they could influence his affections and eventually cause a huge conflict of interests. He should, instead, love his God and not theirs.

4. A King Is Not to Amass Silver and Gold (Deut. 17:17b)

Another area of concern pertains to monetary gain and an overflowing treasury. Ancient kings were well-known for collecting valuable metals and resources through their labor forces, trades with other nations, or gathering the spoils of conquered nations. They would use precious metals for jewelry, currency, architecture, furniture, and as means of payment or even bribery when becoming entangled in diplomatic matters with other kings.

Also, many kings were obsessed with silver and gold, especially because the bigger their treasuries, the more power they were perceived to brandish. Still again, the Lord demands that a king over his people should not collect massive amounts of silver or gold, because there will be no need if the king and the people obey the stipulations of the Mosaic covenant. Nor should the treasury grow to such an extent that a king may be tempted to trust in riches instead of the God who is the creator of all things.

5. A King Must Master the Content of the Law (Deut. 17:18-20)

At this point, we come to somewhat of an awkward stipulation for a king. He is expected to draft a copy of Torah (i.e., the Law) on a scroll provided by the Levitical priests, retain it in his possession during his reign, and read it incessantly to master its content.[47] This sounds reasonable enough since it would be difficult not to become familiar with something that you actually copied yourself. But essentially the king is required to be a scribe and a resident theologian of Israel in Torah studies. There is no mentioning of fighting skills, diplomatic expertise, physical prowess, or emotional temperament. Instead, of all the things that the Lord could mention as primary duties, the king must document the Law himself and become a Torah academician, able to explain its moral demands upon the people.

At first glance, this appears out of place. Yet as we have seen up to this point in OT history, an understanding of the Law is imperative to obedience, and as the Mosaic covenant stipulates, obedience is the key to divine blessing (Ex. 19:5; Deut. 11:1; Josh 1:8). This is why if a king keeps this requirement, he will experience two spiritual outcomes. One is that he will learn about who God is, which means he will understand the values that God's character reflects. Second, he will then innately express an attitude of humility toward the people over whom he rules and together, all of them will experience peace and stability.

Overall, we see that these guidelines cover many of the common practices that ancient success-hungry kings would impulsively want to employ. They would want to have myriads of horses for military might; many wives for pleasure and national alliances; silver and gold to build their treasury; and sustain a massive ego so that the people would fear them and follow their leadership no matter how extreme their demands.

Nevertheless, the Lord's choice of a king would be someone who trusted in divine strength to fight battles, loved one woman who was likewise devoted to the Lord, placed his confidence in the Lord, and was devoted to his Law rather than prideful self-promotion. In light of this, these requirements actually make perfect sense because they direct a king's attention where it belongs, thereby safeguarding him against common temptations that any ancient king would face.

DEUTERONOMY 17 AND THE DAVIDIC LEGACY

When we compare the kingly requirements of Deuteronomy 17 with the recorded history of the Israel's monarchy, it is eye-opening to see how many of the kings were so blatantly disobedient. These kings only served to highlight the need for a better king. We do not have to search far to see the volatile inconsistency of Israel's kings, beginning with David himself.

1. The Life of David

The early years of David's reign began with positive momentum. He brought the Ark of the Covenant back to Jerusalem (2 Sam. 6). He expressed humility after the Lord's promise of blessing on his lineage, as well as competent knowledge of the Lord's faithfulness to Israel in the past (2 Sam. 7:18-29). And he showed mercy to people in need, such as Mephibosheth (2 Sam. 9). David had many traits of the good king that God desired. Of course, we are all too familiar with David's moral collapse, which began with an adulterous relationship with Bathsheba and ended in the cover-up murder of her husband Uriah (2 Sam. 11).

Ironically, Uriah had the character of Deuteronomy 17. When David summoned him from the battlefield, hoping that he would go be with Bathsheba so that her unexpected pregnancy could be attributed to him rather than David, Uriah refused to go home because he deemed it unfair to his men. Why should he get to be with his wife when his fellow Israelite soldiers were still in harm's way? He did not see himself as being above his fellow soldiers. Uriah was so devout that David had to abuse his kingly power by tricking Uriah, making his death appear to be accidental. But the Lord knew better, and he sent Nathan the prophet to confront David (2 Sam. 12:1-15).

In the aftermath of his lapse and restoration, there were a litany of consequences that affected David's immediate family. His baby that Bathsheba bore died (2. Sam 12:15-23); his son Amnon raped his sister Tamar (2 Sam. 13:1-22); his son Absalom then murdered Amnon for committing rape (2 Sam. 13:23-33); and later Absalom tried to usurp the throne from his father David and even went into his concubines on a roof in Jerusalem for all the public to see (2 Sam. 16:20-23). What we see here is that when David chose to violate the Law of the Lord, he withheld from the kingdom tranquility that was promised to the obedient king who obeyed Deuteronomy 17.

2. The Life of Solomon

Like his father, Solomon's reign began with high hopes. We are encouraged by the final words that David shared with Solomon regarding the importance of the Law for success (1 Kgs. 2:1-4). We are rooting for Solomon because of his early request for the Lord to give him wisdom as opposed to power and riches (1 Kgs. 3:3-14). There appears to be a ray of hope for Israel. But like a man lost at sea who watches the helicopter fly overhead without noticing his flares, Israel's hope was shattered.

Solomon eventually made a marriage alliance with a king. This is a bad start by itself. But he did not align with just any king—it was the Pharaoh of Egypt (1 Kgs. 3:1)! Solomon also acquired great wealth for himself (1 Kgs. 4:20-28). But even so, there was still hope. The Lord still promised to give Solomon wealth and power (1 Kgs. 3:10-14, 4:29-34). He was also described as having moral focus because he was driven by a commitment to build (1 Kgs. 5-8). He is also described as exhibiting such moral focus and uncanny wisdom that the Queen of Sheba came to meet him in person. His renown had apparently spread throughout the ancient world (1 Kgs. 10:1-13).

However, like we said, things would go downhill.. As quickly as Solomon had risen to the heights of power and prestige, he began to behave in ways that clearly violated the guidelines of Deuteronomy 17. He began to acquire a massive network of trade with various nations to accumulate commodities, especially gold (1 Kgs. 10:21-22). Solomon also gathered thousands of chariots and horses to such an extent that he had to build actual cities that could store them. And where did he obtain many of the horses for his fleets? You guessed it: Egypt (1 Kgs. 10:26-29).

Finally, Solomon's ultimate downfall came when he decided to marry more and more princesses from other nations. These alliances became so customary that eventually Solomon ended up having some 700 wives and 300 more concubines (1 Kgs. 11:3). The tragic result of such behavior eventually came when Solomon began to pay homage to the deities that his many wives worshiped. He gave deference to some of the most heinous false gods in all of ancient history including Ashtoreth, Milcom, Chemosh, and Molech. He even built pagan altars just east of Jerusalem so sacrifices could be offered to them (1 Kgs. 11:4-8). By the time he had completed his reign, virtually all of the requirements of Deuteronomy 17 had been violated.

3. Surveying Other Kings of Israel

When Solomon's reign came to an end, the requirements of Deuteronomy 17 were met on a hit-or-miss basis, with many more strikeouts than hits. No one was headed to the baseball hall of fame from Team Israel. For instance, Solomon's son Rehoboam inherited the throne and decided to exalt himself as a more powerful king than his father. He listened to the advice of his friends instead of Israel's elders, telling the people that his reign would be much more demanding than his father's. As the king, he should have served his people, not ruled them with an iron fist.[48] Understandably, most of the people revolted against Rehoboam, causing a national split that required the establishment of Jeroboam as a rival king (1 Kgs. 12:1-24). And to make matters worse, Jeroboam turned out to be an idol worshipper and arbitrarily appointed priests who were not Levites (1 Kgs. 12:28-31).

This should not be overlooked because again, if an idolatrous king could appoint priests according to his own liking, then he would probably care less about taking a designated scroll and recording a copy of the Law, as Deuteronomy 17 required. In fact, on different occasions the book of the Law was inaccessible to the nation and possibly even lost. A perfect example of this occurs during the later reign of Josiah. He instilled numerous religious reforms but only after a copy of the book of the Law had been rediscovered (2 Kgs. 22:8-11).

Accordingly, the subsequent story of the Northern and Southern kingdoms is one that tragically ends with the pinnacle curse of the Mosaic covenant—exile from the land. Like their ancient parents, Adam and Eve, who were kicked out of Eden, Israel and Judah are taken separately by pagan nations into captivity, the former being overtaken by the Assyrians in 722 B.C. and the latter being captured by the Babylonians in 586 B.C. Prior to these tragic events, the Northern kingdom never had a devout follower of the Lord as a ruler. The most egregious was King Ahab. He married a Sidonian pagan named Jezebel who became one of the most notorious female characters in all of OT history (1 Kgs. 16:31). He also ruled the people harshly, had his own band of false prophets, and was finally judged by being killed in battle (1 Kgs. 22:29-40).

In contrast, the history of the Southern kingdom did have a few high points. But every time a good king strove to follow the Lord, the following king who was typically corrupt and usually dismantled his efforts. The good kings of Judah included Asa, Jehoshaphat, Joash, Amaziah, Uzziah, Jotham, Hezekiah, and Josiah while the excessively wicked were Ahaz, Manasseh, Amon, and Johoiakim. When we span this time period, again it is amazing to see how many of the priorities of Deuteronomy 17 were either ignored or revived. Idolatry, conspiracies and/or political power plays, and incompetent leadership usually marked the evil kings. They did the very things that Deuteronomy 17 prohibited. On the other hand, kings who exemplified character were known for praying for victory over enemies, emphasizing the corporate responsibility of the people to obey the Law, expressing humility in leadership, and not being consumed with riches or women.

We see that while some rulers honored the kingly guidelines set forth in Deuteronomy 17, these were the exception rather than the rule. Israel's history was largely marked by Davidic descendants who could care less about being the kind of king that God desired the people to have. But the Good King would be worth the wait. God made a promise to Abraham that he intended to keep. Israel's history of bad kings would finally come to an end with the King of Kings.

DEUTERONOMY 17 AND THE GOOD KING

Whereas the Davidic legacy had its few highs and many lows, the NT proclaims that Jesus of Nazareth is the quintessential candidate, consistently meeting all the criteria for Israel's king. Previously many succumbed to idolatry, lust, power, riches, and self-reliance with only a remnant standing out as fearing the Lord.

But consistently Jesus Christ is described as the Son of Man who submitted to his Father and only acted by the power of the Spirit. And in doing so, he exhibited behavior that perfectly aligned with the kingly character that Deuteronomy 17 demanded. He becomes the king to which all other kings will one day bow the knee.

1. Jesus as a Legally Qualified King

For starters, we see that the Gospels place high priority on Jesus's lineage. Why? So that readers can be assured that he was a Davidic descendant, a priority of Deuteronomy 17. We see that Jesus was not accidentally or arbitrarily Jewish.

Both Matthew and Luke provide genealogies tracing Jesus's familial roots back to David and ultimately Abraham (Matt. 1:1ff; Lk. 3:23-38). They also speak of Jesus being born as the King of the Jews (Matt. 2:1-2) and the one who would inherit the throne of David (Lk. 1:32-33). Mark's Gospel focuses upon Jesus's ministry as an exhibition of the Son of Man who proclaims the message of God's kingdom (Mk. 1:14-15). John's Gospel emphasizes that Jesus, as the Son of David, is also the eternal Son of the God who serves as God's new tabernacle amidst his people (Jn. 1:14).[49]

Throughout the Gospels, Jesus often interpreted portions of Davidic psalms as if they were personal journal entries. Though David initially wrote them as he reflected on various life experiences, Jesus saw many of them as prophetic precursors to his own life. In a sense, unbeknown to David, his life as Israel's king served as a script that was later reenacted by the True David when he came to lay final claim to Israel's throne. The early church followed this line of thought by preaching that the kingdom hopes of Israel were now tied to Christ's resurrection and ascension to heaven as the victorious Lord and Davidic Messiah (Acts 2:22-36).

2. Jesus Obeys the Command Regarding Horses

At first glance, there does not seem to be much we can say about Jesus obeying the command for a Davidic king not to amass a large cavalry of steeds. We should remember, however, that this rule was given to prevent Israelite kings from being tempted to trust in their own strength and resources for protection. In that light, we see in the Gospels that Jesus consistently relied on his Father for provisions and defense. We read that he faithfully endured temptation in the wilderness and the Garden of

Gethsemane only to receive aid from angels when the Father chose to send them (Matt. 4:11; Lk. 22:43).

Also, when the band of officers came to arrest Jesus in Gethsemane and bring him before the Sanhedrin, Peter tried to fight against them. Jesus stopped Peter, claiming that he could ask his Father to send twelve legions of angels to intervene (Matt. 26:51-53). But instead of summoning them, Jesus knew it was his Father's will to be vindicated through resurrection in the near future, not through an immediate angelic beat down.

The stunning act of trust is personified in a different way when Jesus entered Jerusalem, a few days before his arrest. As opposed to coming on a mighty steed or in a fancy chariot as a sign of war, he came in peace riding on a young colt with no intent of instigating subversive anarchy or a violent revolution. He was emulating Solomon who also rode a donkey when he came to be inaugurated as Israel's king (1 Kgs. 1:33).[50] And he was fulfilling the prophet Zechariah's earlier prediction that Israel's king would come on a donkey as a sign that God's people would no longer need chariots, horses, or bows because peace would come to the nations (Zech. 9:9-10).

Finally, it is worth noting that when the Book of Revelation describes the return of Jesus to judge the nations, he is portrayed as a conquering king prepared for battle because he rides a horse and is followed by horse-riding heavenly armies (Rev. 19:11-14). However, the scene is anticlimactic because when he rides into battle against the enemies, they are wiped out simply by the word of his mouth because it bears the power of a sword (Rev. 19:21). So even when he has access to heavenly resources, he has no need for them because he is the true King of Kings (Rev. 19:16).

3. Jesus Obeys the Command Regarding Multiple Wives

In contrast to the MTV-like stories of the Davidic kings who either were unfaithful to their wives or married women who served other Gods, Jesus served as the premiere example of fidelity. He remained single during his lifetime and avoided any sexual scandals. He also confronted the issue of adultery (Jn. 4:16-18, 8:3-11) and rebuked those who exploited the practice of divorce (Mk. 10:5-12).

Moreover, according to the NT, the only bride of Christ is made up of the people who he came to redeem. This accords well with the OT theme of Israel as the Lord's spouse because of the Mosaic agreement between them. Israel was God's people and he was their God (Jer. 3:14; Hos. 2:19-20). Now, under the blessings of the new covenant, which abrogate the legalities of the Mosaic Law, the parameters of God's people were expanded through the work of Christ and the Spirit to include both Jews and Gentiles. Therefore, the Church is the bride of Christ.[51] And not only that, Christ's faithfulness to his bride was the Apostle Paul's illustration for how every husband and wife should relate to each other (Eph. 5:22-30).

4. Jesus Obeys the Command Regarding Silver and Gold

We saw earlier that excessive wealth could be the downfall of a king's heart. This is why Deuteronomy 17 insisted that Israel's king should not be consumed with collecting silver or gold. With that in mind, we see that Jesus lived a life that avoided the lure of riches. For instance, Joseph and Mary brought him to the Temple to be circumcised eight days after his birth, as the Law required. They had to offer two birds because they apparently could not afford a lamb (Lev. 12:7-8; Lk. 2:23-24). The heir of the galaxies was born to peasants in a feeding trough, not to royalty in a palace.

Later, in the midst of Jesus's temptations in the wilderness, Satan offered him the kingdoms of the world. He was rejected and dismissed by the Davidic son who would only serve God (Matt. 4:8-10). From then on, Jesus consistently mentioned the fact that if people were going to follow him, they would have to love God more than riches (Mk. 10:17-27). He sometimes told parables that warned against the danger of hording riches. He spoke about how the love of riches chokes one's desire to follow him (Matt. 13:22), blinds people from the true purposes of life (Lk. 12:19-21), and causes people to have tremendous regrets after they die (Lk. 16:19-31).

On other occasions, Jesus said that one must consider the cost in becoming his disciple, because the "Son of Man had no place to lay his head" (Lk. 9:58). Not only that, Jesus at one point even paid a tax by asking Peter to retrieve a shekel from the mouth of a fish (Matt. 17:24-27). In essence, Jesus echoed the priority of Deuteronomy 17 when he asked what a man would profit if he gained the whole world but lost his own soul (Matt. 16:26) or told the masses to seek God's kingdom first and all the things they needed would be added to them (Matt. 6:33). Jesus could have been rich and yet without sin, but he made clear that he was a kingly candidate who was not shaken by allure of wealth.

5. Jesus Obeys the Command Regarding the Law

As we saw earlier in this chapter, the last requirement of Deuteronomy 17 was that a king must produce a copy of the Law on a scroll provided by the Levitical priests. The Gospels do not explicitly record that Jesus did this, but it is clear that his mind was immersed in its content.

For example, Luke records that at twelve years old, Jesus was in the Temple listening to the teachers and asking them questions (Lk. 2:41-46). His inquiries were so perceptive that the people were astounded at his knowledge and answers (Lk. 2:47). Then at the age of thirty, before he began his ministry, he went into the wilderness and as opposed to succumbing to temptation and rebelling the way Israel did, he responded to the Devil's schemes at least three times by quoting books of the Law, namely Deuteronomy (cf., Deut. 8:3, 6:13-16). For the next three years, Jesus constantly appealed to parts of the OT with the famous initial quote, "It is written ... but I say" when he engaged in different matters.

When he quotes Scripture, he exhibits the three basic character qualities ascribed to someone who abides by Deuteronomy 17. First, he revered his Father and observed the words of the Law to the extent that he claimed to have come to fulfill all of it (Deut. 17:19b; Matt. 5). Second, he did not exalt himself above his countrymen. Instead, he humbly identified with those who accepted John's baptism of repentance by being baptized himself (Matt. 3:15). He claimed to have been sent to serve, not be served (Mk. 10:45). He promised to give his life as a ransom for many (Matt. 20:28), and he even illustrated his compassion by washing his own disciples' feet (Jn. 13:1-20). Third, his obedience to the Father resulted in the resurrection which serves as the supreme announcement that all those who follow him will be his sons (heirs) and one day enjoy the establishment of his kingdom (Matt. 26:29; Jn. 1:12).

UNTIL EVERY KNEE BOWS

Jesus is the true Davidic king who meets the kingly demands of the Law. He was a descendant of Abraham, from the tribe of Judah, and a direct member of David's lineage. Beyond having the right DNA, he also exhibited the proper character of Israel's king. He was not concerned about having an excessive number of weapons for any potential war, nor was he distracted by the allures of riches or immoral pleasures. Instead, he was consumed with the will of his Father as well as the words of the Law. He lived a life that personified David's insight that God's law restored the soul and that his judgments were more desirable than gold because they are sweeter than honey (Ps. 19:7-10).

Our King is not some power-hungry bureaucrat in need of judicial oversight. There is no need to wonder if he is bartering with the enemy or seeking to undercut our devotion to him. Our King is the perfect, righteous, reigning Perfect King who serves his people with justice and power. He is the King of Kings because every other king owns land on his turf. As Tim Keller has said, Jesus is not calling us to advice; he is calling us to follow *him*, the king "with power and authority to *do* what needs to be done, and then to offer it to you as good news."[52] When he returns, every knee will bow and every tongue will confess that he is Lord (Phil. 2:10-11).

DISCUSSION

List a few truths you learned in this chapter that you'd not seen in Scripture before.

How do these truths apply to your life?

Why are these truths important to share with others?

7
TEMPLE

In good times and bad, we long to be in the presence of those we love. Whether it is parents with their children, a husband with his wife, or two lifelong friends, we yearn to enjoy life together with the ones closest to us. Because of this, being separated from those we love can be painful, even unbearable. Sometimes life situations such as work or school can require us to live far away from each other, making it difficult to acclimate emotionally to that kind of distance. Estrangement or intense conflict can be even harder to handle.

This kind of separation from a loved one's presence is a major part of the biblical story. The only difference is that the distance is not merely between people—it is between humanity and its Creator. We see this in the opening accounts of the OT where the God of heaven creates the earth and fills it with all of its wonderful features. Anyone who has read other chapters in our book so far knows that Adam and Eve come up often. Well, here they are again! But we have to remember—God's redemption project started there. Creation culminated with the making of two social creatures, a man and woman (Adam and Eve), who were capable of relating to each other and to God himself. At this point, heaven was intimately connected with humanity's place of residence on the earth.

As we have discussed more than once so far, this special bond between heaven and earth was abruptly affected when Adam and Eve defied God's authority. Mankind introduced death to the entire created order and the Lord subsequently declared judgments upon them as well as the earth itself. Furthermore, this wedge between heaven and earth was finally expressed in tragic form when Adam and Eve were banished from the initial place of God's special presence.[53] Yet the story does not end there. After reading about this cosmic rift, the Bible proceeds to tell us how God reestablishes a way for heaven and earth to intersect once again—a way in which these realms could be at peace. And it unfolds by describing how God secured a heavenly address at new earthly locations, beginning with a mountain, then a tent (or a Tabernacle), which eventually transitioned into a building (or a temple), and finally reached its pinnacle form in the person of Jesus himself.

GOD'S PRESENCE IN A GARDEN

The cradle of God's presence with humanity again begins in Genesis 1-2, where we discover two distinct but complimentary accounts of the creation event. Genesis 1 focuses on the well-known creation week, which briefly surveys the basic nuts and bolts of creating the earth, ordering its seasonal functions, and filling it with vegetation and livestock (Gen. 1:1-25). It then concludes with the creation of Adam and Eve, the commission for them to fill the earth and rule over it, and the promise that they could enjoy the nourishment provided by the surrounding trees and plants (Gen. 1:24-2:3).

The key feature to notice at this juncture is the special place that Adam and Eve were given. They were blessed with provisions, delegated with authority over the earth, and privileged to spread God's image throughout the whole earth. In short, Adam and Eve's job was to reflect God's *heavenly* character and power in the *earthly* realm. And they had every opportunity and means to do so.

As we move to the bulk of Genesis 2, we are given more information about how Adam and Eve were to fulfill their Genesis 1 commission. God created a specific garden in Eden somewhere located in the "East." He made it lush with vegetation, full of animal life, and fully supplied with water from a river that ran through the garden and branched off into four others. Even the names of the rivers each represented fruitfulness and abundance. Eden was overflowing with beauty and blessing—it was almost literally heaven on earth.

Also, Eden was somewhat distinct from the rest of the earth for several reasons. For instance, Eden had two trees that had no rival throughout the rest of the earth, namely the tree of the knowledge of good and evil and a tree of life. Likewise, it was in Eden that Adam was placed to begin his work and later received his wife Eve to be his life-long companion. It was even here in Eden where the Lord communed with Adam and Eve. We see examples of this when God brought Eve to Adam to be his wife, as well as when he came to confront them in their sin. And unfortunately, it was ground zero for humanity's judgment because Adam and Eve were kicked out of Eden, forbidden to return.

Before this tragedy, though, Eden again served as the first address shared by the God of heaven and the first two earthly inhabitants. This is why the prophet Ezekiel, for instance, later calls Eden "the garden of God" (Ezek. 28:13) and likens it to God's "mountain" (Ezek. 28:14).[54] It was where heaven and earth met, and yet ultimately parted ways. In many ways, Eden represents the first temple—a place where God dwelled with his people.[55] What's more, its features were not forgotten because centuries later, John in Revelation speaks about heaven actually coming to the earth (Rev. 21-22). He alludes to Eden-like traits of a flowing river from God's throne (Rev. 22:1), the tree of life being available to the nations (Rev. 22:2), the curse of sin no longer having any sway (Rev. 22:3), and creation no longer depending on the sun or moon as before because heaven's new address will be the whole earth (Rev. 22:5). So just as Eden was lost, in a sense it is regained once more. But the question is: How?[56]

GOD'S PRESENCE ON A MOUNTAIN

After sinful humanity went into exile, forfeiting the divine presence in Eden, God began to take all kinds of measures to unite heaven with the earth once again. However, sometimes such a goal required judgment. The earth needed constant baths, so to speak, so that history could be rebooted with a clean slate. The Lord was compelled in one instance to judge all of humanity by bringing the cataclysmic flood in Noah's day, and on another occasion, he destroyed the cities of Sodom and Gomorrah because their wickedness had become so immense. And in another instance, we see the Lord confounding the languages of the people at the Tower of Babel event because they attempted to regain his presence by climbing to the heavens on their own terms instead of submitting to him. So instead of obtaining divine communion by their own power, they actually were forced by God's judgment to do what Adam and Eve were commissioned to do before they sinned—spread out across the earth.

In contrast to the Lord's presence resisting the ongoing evil of humanity, there are many other moments where he expresses his desire to reconcile with his creation. He constantly communicates with believers such as Noah and the great Patriarchs—Abraham, Isaac, and Jacob. He spoke through direct interchanges, dreams, visions, angels, and prophetic utterances. And in response to his interaction with these men, we often see these leaders building altars to praise the Lord because of his various provisions. Such acts not only served as a means of approaching him in worship. They were liturgical landmarks that represented the Lord's presence, because he had accepted the sacrifices that were made on such altars.[57] Even though Eden had been lost, the Lord's presence could still be experienced on his terms of sacrifice and obedience.

Finally, the restoration of the divine presence began to be teased out in covenantal agreements. Specifically, the one he made with Abraham showed how he would restore the nations of the human race by channeling divine blessings through the nation of Israel of which Abraham would be the father. And it is at this point that God's Eden-like presence takes a significant turn. The people of Israel eventually found themselves in Egypt on *positive* terms in the twilight years of Jacob because of his son Joseph's provisionary care. But after that generation of Hebrews left the scene and their population grew, God's people were later enslaved by an evil Egyptian Pharaoh. This set the stage for the Lord to remember his promises to Abraham about a specific land for his promised people, commissioning Moses to lead Israel in the great deliverance of the Exodus. By the time this major event had run its course, the Egyptian deities and authorities had been trounced, the Egyptians were humiliated, their leaders destroyed, and Israel left triumphantly on their way to Canaan. God won. Again. No surprise there.

As they made their way across the Sinai plains, it was there where the Lord then made a covenant with Israel, which included an agreement that his presence would be in their midst. Up to this point, the Lord had shown his presence in miraculous ways. He summoned Moses from a burning bush, which instantly made the ground around it sacred (Ex. 3:4-5). And following Egypt's defeat under the weight of the ten plagues, the Lord used a cloud in the day and a pillar of fire at night to navigate the Hebrew people through the Sinai terrain (Ex. 13:21-22). So, in a sense, he was beginning to manifest his presence for Moses and all of Israel to see.

However, once they made their way to the region of Mount Sinai, the Lord's presence was displayed in an entirely different way. Again, previously Adam and Eve communed with the Lord in the garden as innocent creatures in a right covenantal standing. Now Israel stood on the horizon of receiving a new covenantal agreement. The Lord was going to reinstate his presence among a remnant of humanity. Such a hope emerges early on when the Lord declares, "I will take you as my people, and I will be your God" (e.g., Ex. 6:6-7; 19:5). Notably, he would tangibly abide in Israel's midst, as opposed to any other nations. Even though the Lord cannot be spatially limited to the heavens or the earth, he once again chose to *localize* his presence among a people.

Still, before this promise was fulfilled, Israel received a preview of the sheer power of the Lord's presence. The people were instructed to prepare themselves ceremonially and not approach the mountain without permission. In fact, if any person or animal came too close, they would be killed (Ex. 19:10-15). The Lord promised that within three days, he would "come down" on the mountain. Tall mountains were often considered the homes of divine beings since it was seldom that anyone could climb them.[58] But in this case, Israel had true justification to be in awe. God was coming down the mountain. And on that day, the Lord did not come in the "cool of the day" as he did in Genesis 3. No, it says that the mountain was hidden by smoke and fire as if a giant thunderstorm had taken over its peak. What sounded like a trumpet bellowed, and the mountain shook violently because of the noise of the divine storm. Naturally, the people were terrified.

One can, no doubt, see a key shift in the story of God's presence. In the early parts of Genesis, the divine presence was peaceful, glorious, and tranquil. Here though, it is ominous, overwhelming, even dangerous. The problem is that while God's presence in Eden was something his people (Adam and Eve) could share, now it was something to be guarded so his people (Israel) would not be destroyed. This is clear when the Lord later instructed Moses to let Aaron come up with him, but warned that if the leaders or people came up uninvited, he would "break forth upon them" (Ex. 19:24). Yet if Israel followed the Lord's commands, the beauty of the divine presence could still be seen. We read examples of this when Moses, Aaron, his two sons Nadab and Abihu, and seventy elders of the nation were able to commune with the Lord on the mountain. They shared a meal together on the ground, glistening as though it were made of clear sapphire (Ex. 24:9-11). And later when Moses had to revisit Sinai, he returned down to the people with his face shining because it reflected the glory of God (Ex. 34:29-34).

The dilemma, however, was that Sinai was not Israel's final destination. They were being led to the southern region of Canaan to receive the Abrahamic promise of the land. The pressing concern was this: How could the people behold the glory of the Lord while at the same time being protected from its solar-like brilliance and overwhelming purity? Answer: The divine presence would have to become mobile.

GOD'S PRESENCE IN A TENT

Since everyone knew that Sinai was just a stop along the way to the Promised Land, the Lord gave Moses instructions to build a portable structure where his divine presence could rest as the people continued their journey to Canaan (Ex. 25-31). The same God who had banished the first couple from Eden and almost dismantled Sinai with thunder and fire was now going to condescend to a tent, literally in the midst of the people.

The English word describing this tent with which Bible readers are most familiar is the term "Tabernacle," which means, "dwelling place." God, whose address is the heavenly realm, once again takes up an earthly dwelling place. This highlights the loftiness of God, yet demonstrates his desire to be close to his people.[59] He stands above the heavens with the earth as a footstool, while at the same time having a place where he can commune directly with Israel. The Tabernacle also is referred to as the "sanctuary," meaning that this tent is sacred ground. And in other instances, it is described as a "tent of meeting." Here the stress is on the fact that the Tabernacle (the place where God dwells) or sanctuary (the sacred place) is where the Lord can convene with his people, whether it is Moses, the later anointed Aaronic priests, or certain other individuals.[60]

Israel stayed at Sinai for about a year while in the process of receiving the divine floorplan for this Tabernacle, subsequently building it (Ex. 19:1; Num. 10:11). Upon completion, the Book of Exodus concludes with a dramatic ceremony in which the Lord's consuming glory descended into it. When it was time to move, his glory would rise back into a cloud. This ritual of the Lord camping with the people continued from Sinai to Canaan. As a matter of fact, the Tabernacle was still in existence when King Solomon began to build, although its central piece of furniture, the

Ark of the Covenant, had been moved around a bit during Israel's early history. That being said, if the Tabernacle was God's earthly address during this time of Israel's history, did it somehow reflect his heavenly quarters and if so, how? And also, what were the general purposes of the Lord establishing a new campsite among the Israelites?

1. The Floor Plan of God's Tent

As we mentioned previously, many ancient people thought highly of mountains and gardens. Mountains were revered because they were largely unexplored, being seen as places that only deities could inhabit. And gardens were the envy of many due to their luxurious climates and wealth of farming resources. These scenes were now going to be merged in this Tabernacle-tent. It would reflect—even *store*—the awesomeness of the heavenly glory that was witnessed at Sinai and in Eden.

First, the Tabernacle was to be built with the twelve tribes (except for the Levites since they were the priestly tribe) in specific spots around the tent. In this arrangement, God's presence would be directly in the middle of the nation as a whole. Further, the rectangular compound surrounding the tent entailed a high fence that only had one gate at the eastern wall. This restricted people to enter only from that direction which reflects the similar eastern entrance to Eden (Gen. 3:24).[61]

Unpacking the Tabernacle included seven items that were to be built. For sake of time, we will only mention a few here. Outside the tent in the eastern entry of the Tabernacle complex was a brazen altar where required sacrifices took place. It was the first thing one would see when entering the tent area. It connected directly with the tragedy of Eden—animals had to be slaughtered because Adam and Eve's fig-leaf strategy was not good enough. Only a divinely-delegated substitutionary death would do. No one entered the tent without a clear reminder of the need for a substitute.

Another item with Edenic overtones was found inside the Tabernacle itself. The tent was divided into two partitions. The first room into which the priests entered was the Holy Place, and then past a collection of curtains (a veil) was a second room called the Holy of Holies. God sat here. In the Holy Place, where the priests served, stood a lampstand made of gold with seven candles (six branches). It provided light within the tent's quarters and it was located just outside the room of divine presence, thereby somewhat replicating the function the tree of life in Eden.[62]

Finally, the most important piece of furniture in the Tabernacle was the famous Ark of the Covenant, located within the Holy of Holies. Inside this acacia wood box, which was overlaid inside and out with gold, were not the gruesome demonic spirits from *Indiana Jones*. Instead, it stored key heirlooms of God's provisions for Israel during their journey to Canaan, including the stone tablets of the law that Moses later put there at Horeb, a jar of manna (the heavenly bread that the Lord had given to Israel in the wilderness), and Aaron's staff that actually blossomed (a sign that the Lord had chosen Aaron's tribe to be the priests). On top of the box was the sacred table of atonement, or mercy seat, which was guarded by two installed images of cherubim whose wings covered this sacred place of divine presence.

The angelic guards who watched over Eden's paradise after humanity fell now guarded the Lord's heavenly presence among the Israelites. He did not change. His plan was not finished—and the cherubim were a stark reminder. This was yet another moment in which anyone familiar with the Eden story knew exactly the point God was making.

2. The Role of God's Tent

There were numerous purposes for this Tabernacle's existence, but we only want to emphasize how the Tabernacle maintains continuity with the divine presence theme in the biblical story. Originally, heaven had converged with earth at its inception when humanity was placed in Eden. Then, when that union ruptured, the Lord eventually re-established a new earthly presence among a remnant nation of Adam's children, through whom he would heal other nations. It finally commenced at Sinai, where God made a covenant with his people.

Following this agreement, Israel moved forward with the Lord's presence by their side. Sacred space was now mobile. In a sense, a simulation of Eden (and for that matter, heaven) was now moving with the people to the new land of promise. The Lord's presence returned to his people, but this time in a world wrought with sin. So, the Tabernacle also reminded God's people that while he could approach them, they could not approach him. This is why a means of atonement was provided along with the tent of meeting—the only way the people's sins could be forgiven, and the only way they could be cleansed from the everyday pollution of the fallen world.[63] Just as the Lord covered Adam and Eve's sinfulness in the Garden, now he gave Israel a means of covering their sin in the sacred tent.

GOD'S PRESENCE IN THE TEMPLE

The Tabernacle was the place where God's presence rested from the time of the Canaan conquest to the establishment of the monarchy. It was first installed at Bethel ("House of God") after Israel entered the Promised Land.

This was a region originally identified by Jacob (Israel) as God's house after he saw a vision of angels traversing upon staircases (or a ladder) between heaven and earth.[64] Then later the tent was moved to Shiloh and remained there until the time of Eli the High Priest.

During this time, one misconception that the Israelites came to embrace was that the Ark of the Covenant guaranteed divine blessing. They thought that if they took it into battle, it would automatically ensure a victory. Tragically this was not the case because the ark was eventually taken after a battle with the rivaling Philistines. But just as the Israelites tried to presume upon God's presence and blessing, the Philistines made the mistake of thinking they could control it. What they discovered was that unlike other pagan ancient near eastern deities, the Lord of Israel had home field advantage no matter where the ark was placed. After experiencing a horrendous series of events, the Philistines surrendered the ark and it was stored in Kiriath-jearim.

Some sixty years later, after David finally became the second King of Israel, the Tabernacle was brought to the newly established city of Jerusalem.[65] David placed it in a tent and later planned to build a temple so the Lord's presence could be treated as true royalty, having its own palace in which to dwell. However, David was forbidden to fulfill that task. Instead, his son Solomon completed the project of building the Temple after he became king. When it was finished, the three motifs of God's presence—garden, mountain, and tent—came together in this new structure. The Temple was surrounded by garden-like decorum; it was built on Mount Zion, itself in Jerusalem; and the Tabernacle-tent was placed in the center of the Temple building.

1. The Temple's Purpose and Structure

The Temple highlighted assorted features of God's character. Because architecture is essentially the artwork in which we live, each of the Temple's features was intended to point to the Lord's majesty, sacredness, and power. Just as art is often a visual expression of an idea in creative form, buildings and/or homes typically reflect the personality and status of their residents.[66]

By anchoring the Tabernacle in the Promised Land, it exalted the Lord's faithfulness. Previously, the Tabernacle was the sign that the Lord was going to keep his promises to Israel because he was moving along with them from Egypt to Canaan. Now in the Promised Land, the Temple acted as a means of closure. It was fixed on Mount Zion in the capital city. It represented security, stability, and safety because the Lord lived among the people at a permanent address. Furthermore, because the Temple was where the Lord dwelt, it was the place where heavenly decisions were made—not just for Israel's fate but the surrounding nations as well (cf., Ps. 29:10; 99:1-5; Amos 1:1-15). Zion was the center of the world—not literally in some geographical sense, but theologically because everything was under the Lord's authority. The Lord's Oval Office was now the Temple.

We would be remiss, however, to stop with the observation that the Temple reflected God's character and authority. It also mirrored his heavenly habitat and was built to provide a visual aid illustrating the otherworldly nature of heaven. But the only way an earthly structure could achieve such a goal was if it replicated previous encounters between heaven and earth. This is why much of the Temple was overlaid in gold, riddled with carvings of trees and flowers, and filled with cypress and olive wood. It was, in a sense, a cubicle version of a garden. At the same time, it maintained continuity with the Tabernacle because its inner chambers were placed in the Temple. And to top it off, the Temple again was established on Mount Zion, which made it just as sacred as Sinai, where the Lord originally married himself to Israel.

It also pictured the God's rule over creation by instilling two enormous cherubim standing side-by-side with their wings touching each other. The image conveyed was that of a kind of seat where the Lord sat over creation, with the ark being his footstool.[67] The Temple was a kind of microcosm of heaven that touched down in the Promised Land among the earthly people of Israel.

2. The Temple's History

At this point, it is easy to see why the Temple was central to Israel's understanding of God and their identity as his people. Unfortunately, the nation applied their previous distortion of the Ark of the Covenant to the Temple. They believed that the mere possession of the building ensured God's blessings. However, the Temple (just like Eden, Sinai, and the Tabernacle) only harbored special status when the Lord chose to reside in it. And his presence was contingent upon obedience to the covenantal obligations that were documented in the Law. Israel was to abide by this divinely-received constitution in order to be in a right standing before the Lord. If the Law was violated without pending repentance or atonement, it listed various curses that could fall upon the people, with exile from the Promised Land as the pinnacle of judgments. This ended up being the exact fate of Israel in 587 B.C. The Babylonian armies invaded Jerusalem, destroyed Solomon's temple, and uprooted many of the Jews to take them back to Babylon as captives. Banishment from the Promised Land was indicative of a dire reality—God's presence had departed from the Temple.

Still, we cannot stop there, because God did not stop there. The promise of judgment was never the final word. He did not abandon his people. Following his standard m.o., the Lord extended the promise of blessing and restoration. We see this good news arriving after the demise of the Babylonian empire and the rise of the Persians. King Cyrus the Great permitted the Israelites to return to their homeland. During three major phases of exiles returning to the Promised Land, the Israelites were able to rebuild their lives, which included restoring another temple. This was a display of God's faithfulness to Israel, no doubt, because he has promised that the glory of this new temple could supersede that of Solomon's (Hag. 2:4-9).

For a while, this renewed focus on the Temple panned out well. Many of the earlier prophets like Isaiah and Jeremiah, as well as the current prophets like Ezekiel, Daniel, and Zechariah all spoke about the restoration of Israel. Yet as history records, the Jewish people once again began to violate their covenantal obligations. This resulted in constant conflicts with surrounding nations, which ultimately ended in the desecration of the Temple during the Maccabean revolt.

Subsequent conflicts maintained political tensions, especially during the early stages of the later Roman Empire's growth. By the time history approached the birth of Christ, the Temple was in such need of repairs that the King Herod the Great had it completely renovated and expanded. The problem, though, was that the Jews did not control the Temple nor did they have power over their land. They were exiled in their own neighborhoods under the thumb of the Romans, awaiting the divine presence

THEY SPOKE OF ME

to vindicate them and reconvene harmony between heaven and earth. This expectation helped set the stage for the ministry of Christ.

JESUS AS THE NEW TEMPLE

The future prospect of God's renewed presence among his people always remained central to the Jewish faith. But by the time Jesus came on the scene, the Temple had become somewhat of an irony. It was a visible reminder of everything absent from Israel's hope. Although it stood atop Jerusalem, there was no airtight control over the priesthood, no Davidic king who ruled from Jerusalem, no control over Israel's borders. On the one hand, the Temple was a landmark testament to God's faithfulness to Israel because once again it represented his presence. Still, on the other hand, it triggered a certain amount of bewilderment because there were so many things that the Lord's presence had not accomplished. By this time, it was both a source of hope and disappointment.

It was this crisis of faith that helped create the volatile setting into which Christ was sent. Israel wanted to know that the Lord's temple-presence would one day address all of their concerns.[68] And this is partly why we see the Gospels immediately applying divine presence language to Christ. For example, in Matthew's account of the angelic announcement Christ's birth, he claims that his arrival marked a fulfillment of Isaiah's prophecy that a son would be born named Immanuel, meaning "God with us." We also see in Luke's account of Jesus's birth that angelic hosts proclaimed to nearby shepherds that the God of the *highest* (or the heavenlies) had brought peace to the *earth*. Luke also recounts Jesus's circumcision where he was brought to the Temple in Jerusalem. A man of

God named Simeon held him, declaring that the baby was the Lord's salvation, which he was accomplishing in the "presence" of the people, both Jew and Gentile. From here, the Gospels continue to expand this theme of Jesus as the divine temple-presence in various ways. Let us focus on just two that are most emphatic in the NT.

1. Jesus Was a Walking Temple

A good place to start is the tension between what the Temple was *supposed* to be and who Jesus *actually* was. As we have seen, it was intended to be the Lord's permanent address among his people. He had communed with Adam and Eve in Eden. He had bonded with the Israelites at Sinai and in the Tabernacle. He resided with the nation in the land of promise via the Temple. Now the arrival of Jesus marked a new chapter in this story. He was the divine presence in mobile-human form.

We see this point, for example, in John's Gospel. Here, Christ is portrayed not as deity clothed in a dark cloud over a mountain, or a Tabernacle room shrouded in fabrics, but as God in the flesh. He came in human form to "dwell" or "tabernacle" among the nations—Israel in particular and the Gentiles in general (John 1:14). And instead of watching the glory of God from afar at the bottom of Sinai or by proxy through the eyes of the high priest, John says that everyone was able to see his "glory." People were able to hear his teachings and see his miracles. We even catch a glimpse of the power of God's presence once more when the Jewish authorities came to arrest Jesus in the Garden of Gethsemane. John claims that when Jesus said he was the one they were seeking, they drew back and fell to the ground (John 18:6). When their motives were exposed by the gravity of his presence, they literally collapsed in trepidation.

The Transfiguration was another dramatic example of Christ being a walking temple. Jesus went up on a mountain with Peter, James, and John where he then revealed the glory of the divine presence.[69] Yet unlike Moses, Jesus possessed the divine glory within himself, reflecting the same divine aura of his Father. His face glowed like Moses's did, just not for the same reason; the divine glory shone from the inside out instead of merely reflecting an external source. So as opposed to a portable tent being carried across the wilderness or a temple fixed on a mountain, the divine presence was now encased in a human being. The Son was a living, breathing temple. The Lord's address between heaven and earth was transitioning from Mount Zion to the heavenly Son who had come to earth.

Now at first glance, one would assume that such a reality would inspire hope, and for some it did. But for others, this connection between Jesus and the Temple raised serious concerns. Why? Because some Jews found it difficult to see the expected Messiah as a new temple when Herod's temple was still standing in Jerusalem. This dilemma caused quite a divide between Jesus and the religious leaders of his day, because the Temple was their political bread and butter. We see this conflict rising on at least two fronts. First, tensions rose when Jesus occasionally claimed to be greater than the Temple. Jesus contended that his position as the Son of Man (or the heavenly agent of his Father's kingdom) gave him authority to (1) indict those who misunderstood the purpose of the Temple, and (2) transcend its importance. In other words, what the Temple originally did, he could do supremely better. If this were true, the religious leaders would be put out of business. No more money-changing. No more extortion. No more leverage.

This led to the other part of the impasse between Jesus and his opponents, which was his shocking prediction that Temple would be destroyed. This bold claim appeared to be an affront to Israel's hopes, but in reality it was a charge of divine judgment against the Jerusalem's corrupt leaders. Jesus was essentially saying that they were going to be cut off because of their lack of spiritual integrity. Note here that the Temple itself was not the problem. On the contrary, as a faithful Jew, Jesus held it in high esteem. His zeal for the Lord's dwelling place was so fervent that at least on one occasion he forcefully dispersed the moneychangers from the Temple because they had made it into something it was never supposed to be. It was intended to be a light to the nations and a house of prayer to the one and true living God. Instead, it had become a strip mall for bartering, trade, and possibly even corrupt business deals. While Jesus claimed that it would be sacked, he still revered its role in Israel's heritage.

What balanced out his respect for the Temple with his declaration of its demise was the fact that the covenantal agreement undergirding its existence (the Mosaic covenant) was being phased out. Jesus, as the new source of the divine presence, was ushering in a new covenant. This is why he occasionally alluded to himself as a temple because, in a sense, he was reliving the Temple's story. Just as God's enemies had destroyed the Temple, so would the corrupt leaders of Israel and the Roman authorities put him to death. And just as it had been defiled, so would a son of perdition (namely Judas) betray the Son of Man to unjust leaders.

2. Jesus Surpasses the Tabernacle/Temple's Functions

Jesus's fulfillment of the various services that the Temple provided is the second major NT emphasis. An immediate case in point is the frequent allusions between the furniture of the Tabernacle-Temple and Christ himself. For instance, early on in the book of Revelation, Jesus is the one, like a Levitical priest in the Tabernacle, who walks among the candlesticks. Yet instead of watching over the Temple's furniture, he now inspects his people—the Church.[70] He also is the one who gives the Holy Spirit so people can worship the Father regardless of their geographic location. The day was coming when bickering over the sacredness of Mount Zion (for the Jews) or Mount Gerazim (for the Samaritans) would be irrelevant (John 4:19-23). Also, the sacred Holy of Holies was vacated and the dividing veil was torn in two because Christ made a way in which sinners could approach heaven itself, rather than taking a trip to an earthly embassy.

Finally, the Temple's location as the place where atonement and forgiveness of sin could be obtained was key. By following the sacrifices that were documented in the Law, which culminated in the annual Day of Atonement, the Temple was the spot where Israel could have their sin problem addressed. The only hitch, as the Book of Hebrews makes clear, is that it could only enforce the benefits of the Mosaic covenant. This meant that Temple sacrifices were ongoing, not permanent. Likewise, the numerous laws against ceremonial uncleanness also safeguarded sacrifices. One may not even qualify to approach the Temple if these rules were being broken. But Christ overcame both of these barriers.

When it came to uncleanness, the problem was that it could be transferred from person to person, but cleanness could not—unless Jesus was involved. He could touch lepers and make them whole, heal physical deformities, cast out demons, and raise the dead. He was able to absorb the filthy wretchedness of uncleanness and still remain clean. Even beyond that, he himself established a titanium steel covenant where a day of atonement only had to occur one time (Heb. 7:27; 10:10). And once it did, the mercy seat of the divine presence was triumphantly replaced by a Messiah who now sits on the heavenly throne as the resurrected Lord.

THE FINAL TEMPLE

The story of the Temple is about how the God of heaven established an earthly address with his people. Whether it be in Eden's garden, the later mountain of Sinai, the humble Tabernacle tent, or Solomon's grand wonder on Mount Zion, each of these locations were proof that the Lord desired to restore his presence among broken sinners. But as glorious as they all were, they served as mere precursors to the final manifestation of God's presence, which was Christ himself.

Jesus permanently bridges the gap between heaven and earth. He reconciles sinners to the Father. And he is the one who will on day bring heaven's domain to the earth so that their locations will be one and the same. He became the Temple, cleansed the Temple, through the Holy Spirit makes us all temples, and will one day renew creation so the earth itself will be a temple.

Therefore, we do not have to long for the presence of our Lord. We do not have to go anywhere to meet with God, because he lives within us. We are living temples, carrying with us the God who saves sinners. So not only should we praise God for his grace and mercy. We should show others how the divine presence can indwell them as well.

DISCUSSION

List a few truths you learned in this chapter that you'd not seen in Scripture before.
How do these truths apply to your life?
Why are these truths important to share with others?

8
PSALMS

Many of us enjoy keeping a diary because we can express ourselves freely and privately. It serves as a safe haven where we can flesh out our thoughts on paper (or a screen) as a kind of self-induced therapy. And when we do so, we write about all kinds of things. Sometimes we just like to reminisce about the idle moments of a regular day. At other times, we enjoy basking in good memories with friends or briefly reliving a mountaintop moment that we recently had. We can even vent our frustrations with personal shortcomings, other people, or difficult situations that never seem to end. Or at a deeper level, there are moments where we reflect on our deepest hurts and regrets. It is often that these moments make diaries a compendium of sacred pages. They are not only marked with heartfelt words. Some of them are tear-stained as well because of previous struggles we endured which we rarely, if ever, share with others. Yet regardless of our motives for writing each entry, a completed journal leaves behind a testimony of our innermost feelings about the flurry of experiences we go through in a lifetime.[71]

When we approach the OT, we discover that the Book of the Psalms (or the Psalter) also serves as a kind of journal. It is a collection of private reflections, poetic discourses, theological assessments, and prayers that the authors expressed in light of their personal dealings with the Lord. At the same time, these ancient journal entries retain two key differences from diaries today. One is that only the people who own them write modern journals. Today we do not talk about collective diaries where a single volume contains personal entries from different writers who can have access to what other contributors have said. Such a book would negate any possibility of privacy, thereby nullifying the main purpose of a journal. But whereas we view a journal as belonging to one person, the Psalms are not like that. Numerous people recorded them and their "entries" collectively serve as running commentary on Israel's experiences with the Lord. While they share some of the same content that we discuss in our journals, their input was to be handed down to future generations of Israelites.

The other key difference between Israel's Psalms and current journals pertains to how Jesus and NT writers used them. Typically, when people write in their journals today, they reflect on things about their past or the present or they may express their hopes for the future. However, no one writes about the future in the past tense. Put another way, no one meditates on feelings and life events before they happen. That would be nonsensical—unless we are talking about Christ himself. As Israel's national archive of worship entries, he often saw the Psalms as predictive in nature. They were perceived as a kind of collective pre-script that he was living out. While they were originally produced in the contexts of the ancient authors' life experiences, Jesus then replicated them in various ways during key moments of his earthly ministry. In a sense, then, events in his life were written before they happened. And it is here where we can see many fascinating connections between the Savior and the Psalms.

WHAT ARE THE PSALMS?

For many believers, the Book of the Psalms holds a special place in their hearts. The main reason is that there seems to be a kindred spirit shared between the Psalmists and readers. For example, the Psalter confesses many of the same struggles we face. He sometimes confesses his sins, acknowledges his weaknesses, and pleads for the Lord's forgiveness. During these moments, we feel as if the Psalter has eavesdropped on our own conversations with the Lord.

Likewise, the writers pose the same kinds of questions that we still ask today. Probably the most common: "God, where are you?" Like the Psalmist, we are aware of God's promises to deliver his people, but the Lord appears to take his sweet time coming to our rescue. Regardless of the subject matter, though, we are gripped by these ancient poems because of their ability to use language in such penetrating and beautiful ways. Moreover, there are several common features of the Psalms that are important to keep in mind if we want to understand how Israel read them, and how Jesus and later NT writers reflected on them. Four are worth mentioning here.

1. Psalms Are Poetry Put to Music

For starters, one major reason the Psalms' words are so moving is because they were literary pieces frequently set to music. We know this initially from the fact that the actual title "Psalms" is an English transliteration of the Greek title *Psalmoi*, which is the book's opening inscription in the Septuagint (a Greek translation of the OT). The term refers to words that were sung to melodies produced by stringed instruments. It is also a Greek equivalent for a Hebrew word *mizmor*, which is used periodically throughout the Psalms to refer to songs set to music. Further, the original Hebrew title ascribed to these writings was a word meaning *to praise* or *praises*. In other words, they represented Israel's corporate hymnbook, or liturgical playlist.[72]

We have all had a song stuck in our heads for days on end, and we are amazed at times that we can remember song lyrics from a song we have not heard in years. We love some because of the music that accompanies them, others because of the specific message they convey, and some for a special memory that a song triggers in our minds. Similarly, Psalms were written amidst a host of life situations. Some were written during low times of desperation. Others were documented to express great joy and celebration. Still some were put to verse as general prayers that all of God's people could emulate. We have songs that resonate with us today; likewise, Israel had the Psalms at their disposal. As Israel's ancient songwriters, the Psalmists produced a collection of songs that the nation could sing corporately in their worship together and individuals could recite or pray in their most private moments. The Psalter was Israel's greatest hits collection.

2. Psalms Are Written by Different Authors

Second, the Psalms are written by an assortment of writers, or lyricists. Most readers are familiar with the fact that David, the second king of Israel, wrote many of them. In fact, over seventy are attributed to him and take up almost the entire first two books (or collections) of the Psalms.[73] This is why he's known as the "sweet Psalmist of Israel" (2 Sam. 23:1). The remaining three books are a collection of Psalms written by various authors such as Solomon, the sons of Korah, Asaph, and one even possibly by Moses. What we see then is that the Psalms were writings that accumulated over Israel's history. They are, again, like journal entries that were preserved through the years, and became a memorable and reflective authority for the people. They represented Israel's conversations with the Lord—conversations that echoed from one generation to the next.

3. Psalms Are the Liturgy of Israel

A third major trait of the Psalms is that they document Israel's expressions of worship, prayer, and theology. This is largely why the Psalms serve as a cumulative hymnbook for the nation—they merge the gap between theory and practice. The authors share their thoughts about who God is, based on disclosures he has made in the past. Israel is then invited to follow their lead as they worship the Lord in prayer and praise.

Further, we could say that while the Law told Israel what the Lord wanted them to do and the prophets instructed them on what to expect, the Psalter synthesizes these resources so Israel could learn how to converse with the Lord. Essentially, then, they were confessional or liturgical treatises. They are confessional because they assert things about God's nature and how he interacts with the world. They are liturgical because they are functional scripts which can be re-quoted because they draw people into worship. The words create a roadmap of shared experiences as God's people, whether it be ancient Israel or those in Christ today. Just as songwriters and musicians who are able to encapsulate our feelings in such penetrating and captive ways, so also the Psalter is able to teach us how to engage the Lord in ways that we cannot always express on our own.

4. Psalms as Dialogue

Finally, a fourth common factor for the Psalms is they *describe*, not merely prescribe, how one should talk with God. In some ways, this is what endears us to the Psalms the most. The authors allow themselves to be vulnerable; they not only wrestle with the Lord over their doubts, fears, and failures, but they graciously record them for future generations to read. This is why we embrace them today with a sense of solidarity.

For example, we feel David's desperation when he pleads for forgiveness in Psalm 51; we resonate with the dark despair of the Sons of Korah in Psalm 88; and we echo Asaph's frustration with God's justice in Psalm 72. But even beyond our connections with their words, the authors show us how to wrestle with God in a worshipful way. They display the perspectives and transparency that are essential to robust prayer and faith. Likewise, they are able to say things about the Lord that are not always acceptable in other literary genres. The rules of the Psalms, like journals, allow the writers to complain, plead, and even argue to an extent. This is permissible, though, because the Psalms are recording how people feel—good, bad, or ugly—in light of what they rightly know. In essence, the Psalmists plead with the Lord to help them figure out how what they know in theory corresponds with their everyday lives.

WHAT KIND OF PSALMS ARE IN THE COLLECTION?

Part of the Psalms' charm is their diversity. No Psalm can talk about everything, just as no single journal entry or song can. It takes all kinds of Psalms to cover the multifaceted questions and struggles that come along with living and breathing in a fallen world. Similar to a good country music album, there really are several ways to complain about the same exact thing. Thus, when we read the Psalms, it is important to notice some of the more common themes that the authors emphasize.[74]

In true human form, a large chunk of the Psalms features lament. We are not happy all the time. And when pain overcomes us, we normally ask the most soul-searching questions. In some instances, the Psalmists express their grief in terms of pleas for vindication instead of mourning or depression. There are even times when the authors explicitly ask the Lord to enact judgment against their enemies. We call these imprecatory Psalms.

But when we think about prominent motifs in the Psalms, we normally gravitate toward the idea of praise or thanksgiving. We might quote Psalm 150 because of its stress on praising the Lord in all kinds of ways, whether with dancing, musical instruments, or simply the breath in our lungs. Some other related themes that surface regularly in the Psalms are expressions of thanksgiving, praise, and celebration. Many times, the Psalter is overcome with joy in light of how the Lord has shown his faithfulness, protection, and favor. In this vein, like lament Psalms, they can be personal or corporate. In addition, the Psalmists know that the Lord is not only to be worshipped for what he does or can do, but also for who he is.

Joined with these Psalms are also various songs of celebration. Again, these pieces are written ultimately for the benefit of Israel as a nation, not just individuals. At times, there were moments where public festivities were in order, so there are Psalms that were appropriate for specific occasions. Some encouraged God's people to renew their commitments; others commemorated God's faithfulness as ruler over the earth; some honored the Davidic king; and still some became popular to sing in worship on Mount Zion.

Finally, another cluster of related Psalms that are distinctive entail those that focus on history, wisdom, and confidence. Specifically, the first set pertains to Psalms that reflect on God's dealings with Israel in the past. Sometimes the Psalter recounts times when the Lord intervened for the nation's sake and is reminded that the Lord will be as faithful as ever. There are other moments where the Psalter wants to reflect on life in general so he can persuade his readers to learn from the past to avoid future pitfalls. And lastly, there are occasions where Psalmists simply want to stand before God to confess their confidence in him regardless of their circumstances.

Together, the Psalms cover many of the basic stages of a life; not just an individual one, but an entire nation's. The Psalms are not a story about random people with random circumstances—they record the experiences of God's chosen people as they strive to understand and obey him. Their hope is that the Lord will be with them and fight for justice. They are trusting that the Lord will do this. However, their life experiences don't always match their hopeful expectations. Thus, the litany of questions in the psalmists' minds: Dare we hope? How, O Lord? When, Lord? And yet, our ability to empathize with their angst always draws us back to the book's pages. But the question still remains, who can finally bring all of their lament and praise to a final conclusion?

THE PSALTER AS CHRIST'S DIARY

When we leap forward to the NT, we see Jesus alluding to all sorts of OT texts. Sometimes he quotes the prophets as an indictment on certain people for their rebellion or spiritual dissonance (e.g., Isaiah, Hosea, Jonah). On other occasions, he quotes sections of the Pentateuch (especially Exodus and Deuteronomy) to correct people's misconstrued views of the Law. But alongside these teachings are his allusions to the Psalms.

Again, keeping in mind that they were the ancient song list for Israel, Jews were familiar with them. It makes perfect sense that Jesus would regularly quote them. But as we read the occasions where he chose to cite them, we discover a unique dynamic. For the people of Israel, the Psalms included a host of activities from prophetic statements to prayers and worshipful lyrics. For Christ, though, they served as his diary that was written in advance. How could this be? The answer is that royalty—King David himself—produced many of the Psalms.[75] He wrote out of his experiences as the ruler of God's people in God's chosen kingdom. When David prayed for deliverance from his enemies, asked for forgiveness, or praised the Lord for his greatness, he did so as the anointed ruler of the divinely chosen nation. And as we saw in a previous chapter, David was not to be the eternally established ruler of Israel. He was just the biological point of reference for a later descendant.

Therefore, when Jesus arrived on the scene, he rightfully inherited the Davidic overtones of the Psalms. Think about it this way: David thought he was writing his own spiritual diary in the Psalms, but he was actually creating a future script for the Son of God to fulfill centuries later. The Psalms of David were essentially Christ's biography written in advance.

They were a compilation of his life experiences that corresponded to Christ's life. Let's look at a few examples.

1. Jesus as a Stumbling Block (Psalm 118:10)

A good starting point that illustrates this solidarity between the Psalms and Jesus is found in an interchange that he had with the chief priests and elders during the passion week. In all three of the Synoptics (i.e., Matthew, Mark, and Luke), the authors record some heated discussions that Jesus had with these religious leaders in the Temple area shortly after his triumphant entry into Jerusalem. The initial portion of their disputes was instigated when Jesus had cleansed the Temple and captured the attention of the crowds with his teachings. Because of his immediate notoriety, the religious leaders could neither arrest nor have him killed publicly. So, they decided to question his authority. Their strategy was if they could discredit him then his words and antics in the Temple would be irrelevant. He could be discarded as just another disillusioned revolutionary.

This strategy ended up backfiring, because when they asked Jesus about the authority upon which his actions and words were based, he countered with a question about John the Baptist's authority. Both Christ as well as the religious leaders knew there was no politically correct or neutral answer to this question. If they affirmed John's ministry, they would indict themselves because they ignored his message of repentance. But if they openly dismissed John, they would plummet in the polls because the people respected John as a prophet. This impasse led to further points that Christ wanted to make about their rejection of his ministry. He told several parables to expose their underlying evil motives and assure them that judgment would fall if they failed to repent. And in the process, Jesus alluded to Psalm 118 as a reference to the kind of rejection that the religious leaders were enacting against him.

The Psalm speaks of an Israelite, possibly a king (or even David himself), who was being oppressed by surrounding nations (Ps 118:10). He was inviting Israel to praise the Lord with him because he had been delivered from these unidentified enemies. In the midst of his worship, he then appeals to a building metaphor to illustrate the Lord's faithfulness. While the surrounding nations treated him (and most likely Israel as a corporate whole) as a stone to be thrown away instead of used for construction, the Lord reversed his plight. But not only did he make the Psalmist a useful stone. He turned him into a corner stone, or the primary stone that held other stones together. Now, in similar fashion, Jesus was claiming that the Psalmist's exclamation was indicative of what the Father was going to do. The only difference was that now the surrounding nations of the ancient Psalm were now replaced by Jewish unbelievers, and the vindicated rock was going to be the very Messiah who they were rejecting. What we can see then is that just as the Psalmist, a representative of Israel, was delivered by the Lord instead of being discarded by his enemies, so would Christ be vindicated by his Father and bring salvation to any Israelite (or Gentile) who identified with him.[76]

2. Jesus as the Suffering Savior

Many of the Psalms express pleas for God's rescue. Sometimes the difficulties are consequences of sin that the Psalmist is facing. On many other occasions, David cries out to God as Israel's enemies are quickly approaching. This leads to urgent requests for the Lord to do something before it is too late. And we see in the Gospels that such Psalms create an archive to which Christ appeals, especially as he is opposed by Israel's religious leaders and later executed as a sacrificial substitute for humanity's sin.

a. Psalms 35:19 and 69:4

An immediate example of this can be seen in the connection between Psalms 35:19 and 69:4. In the first reference, David records v.19 in the context of a request for the Lord to turn the tables on his enemies (35:8). They were opposing him for no good reason (35:7) and even seeking to take his life (35:4). If that was not enough, they were doing all of this even though he had extended mercy to them in the past (35:12-15). This is why, at one point, David asks the Lord to prevent his enemies from being victorious because they hate him "without a cause" (35:19).

Similarly, in Psalm 69, David starts off with the same request for God's deliverance because his enemies are so numerous. In this Psalm, though, David feels like he is drowning in an ocean with no bottom (69:2), his throat is even parched because he has cried out for so long (69:3). He then repeats the point of 35:19—his many enemies hate him without a just reason (69:4). Together, these passages are illuminated when Jesus warns his disciples about the inevitable hatred that is awaiting them. Simply put, just as Jesus was being rejected and soon to be killed, so would they. But then he makes the further point that the Scriptures themselves promised suffering for them, specifically in David's claim that God's people are resisted without cause (John 15:25). King David's enemies persecuted him, which was a prelude to those who would assault his Messianic descendant and eventually all his followers as well.

b. Psalm 41:9

A second example of how the Psalms relationship with Christ's sufferings can be found in the sad situation of Judas' betrayal. While in the upper room to share one last Passover meal with his disciples, Jesus claims that one of them will betray him. The disciples are initially bewildered by such a charge. Oddly, in Matthew's rendition, Judas actually incriminates himself by asking if it is him (Matt. 26:25) and Mark records that Jesus tells them it is the one who would soon dip food in a bowl with him (Mark 14:20). In John's account, we are given a bit more information. We discover that John was prodded by Peter to get to the bottom of the matter by asking Jesus who the traitor was. When he did, John was informed that it would be the one to whom Jesus would give a morsel of food, Of course, it was Judas (Jn. 13:26-27).

Yet before this private conversation took place, Jesus had already made the point that his promise was for eleven, not twelve. He then quotes Psalm 41:9, which speaks of a friend with whom he eats, who later raises his heel against him (John 13:18). In this Psalm, David spoke about his enemies who were kind in his presence but ruthless behind his back (Ps. 41:5-8). David's situation was so toxic that even a close friend turned his heel against him. Jesus saw this event in David's life as indicative of his. Judas had followed him for three years only to betray him in the end. And to make matters worse, Jesus quoted this Psalm right after he had humbly washed his disciples' feet, including their heels.

c. Psalm 22

Psalm 22 also plays a significant role in the Gospels' descriptions of Christ's death. The original tone of the Psalm is immediately set in the opening verse, where David desperately asks the Lord why he has forsaken him. He thinks the Lord is ignoring his groans and cries for help. To make matters worse, David knows that the Lord has come through for his people before in times of trouble (22:3-4). So why is he not helping now? From here, the rest of the Psalm wavers back and forth between David's descriptions of his suffering at the hands of his enemies and his underlying confidence that God will deliver him. And it is David's grieving that reflects the exact tone that is set at Jesus's crucifixion.

Further, John 22 highlights a parallel between the antics of David's ancient enemies and the Roman soldiers who crucified Jesus. David had claimed that his enemies surrounded him like a pack of rabid dogs with the intent of killing him. He felt as if they had pierced him so they could enjoy watching him slowly die (22:16-17). Then to celebrate their victory, David said they chose to gamble over his remaining garments (22:18). Now jumping forward to Jesus's execution, remember that John records this as an eyewitness. He, not Jesus, makes the connection between David's account and what he saw the Roman soldiers doing at the scene of the cross. They were greedily casting lots to determine who could have Jesus's tunic. John quotes Psalm 22:18 as another Davidic allusion that reflected Jesus's life (Jn 19:24). But it should be pointed out that Jesus's experiences were not the only things corresponding to the prayerful liturgies of the Psalms. Sometimes the actions of his enemies did, too.

Another more emphatic link with Psalm 22 emerges during Jesus's last moments. For example, he spoke of how his enemies mocked him because the Lord had not appeared to save the day (22:8). David said that they jeered with as much aggression as ravenous lions. If they could, they would devour him as he faded away in despair (22:13-15). In like manner, all of the Synoptic Gospels mention how the religious leaders ridiculed Jesus, demanding that he save himself. Though unstated, it is possible that Jesus looked upon this spectacle through the lens of Psalm 22. His enemies hurled insults, his body was pierced, and he felt abandoned; all of this reflecting David's original descriptions of whatever plight he had endured.[77] It was, in fact, as if Jesus were encountering Israel's ultimate curse, which was exile. But rather than being displaced from the Promised Land, he was being deserted by his Father. This is why he bursts in emotion by quoting the opening of the Psalm, which is famously known as his cry of dereliction, "My God, My God, why have you forsaken me?" (Matt. 27:46; Mk. 15:34; Lk. 23:35-39) Like David, even though Jesus knew that the Lord was faithful to deliver, he cried out in his immediate emotional agony because his rescue was not to come at that moment.[78] One could safely deduce then that Psalm 22 was a major part of the ancient screenplay for Jesus's death.

3. Jesus as the Victorious King

Another set of Psalms that are critical to Jesus's self-understanding are ones that speak of Israel's king having authority over the nations of the earth. David, again, wrote most of them since he was the king with whom the Lord made a covenantal agreement. David was assured that eventually his "son" would inherit Israel's throne and receive the Lord's authorization to exercise divine justice worldwide. There are numerous Psalms that speak in such terms and once more, these Davidic overtones of sonship are expanded significantly in the NT. God's original promises regarding David's physical line are still retained—a true descendent would be the rightful king. Nevertheless, this Davidic son will also be the divine Son (or Son of Man) who is sent from heaven. In a real sense, the Lord (God the Son) becomes the Lord (glorified Davidic King). More specifically, the NT interprets various Psalms in light of Jesus's role as the resurrected Christ who has ascended to heaven as Israel's victorious Savior. And the two that convey this point the most are Psalms 2 and 110.

a. Psalm 2

In the second Psalm, the author (perhaps David) exalts the status of Israel's king and cautions other nations about defying his authority, equating it to disobeying the Lord himself. The Psalm opens with the claim that the surrounding nations have no desire to concede. They are in an uproar because they view the Lord's anointed as a tyrant who will shackle them with oppressive cords. The Psalter then says that God is humored by such antics and makes it clear that his king is established on Mount Zion to rule over the nations with the earth as his spoils. Furthermore, he will reign with a rod of iron, which can crush any resistant nation like old pottery. But as an extension of mercy, the Psalter concludes with an admonition: if the nations show reverence to the Son, they will find refuge from his wrath.

Now this tension between the nations and the Lord's anointed king becomes a key theme after Jesus's resurrection. Many now reject this newly resurrected Lord, who has ascended to heaven and awaits his return to judge the world. His gospel message, which is being declared by his disciples, is being viewed by many Gentiles as senseless and by Jews as offensive. They are railing against God's anointed just as the Psalmist declared they would (cf., Acts 4:25-26; Rev 11:15-18). Likewise, even Jesus in his glorified state alludes to this Psalm when he revealed himself to John on the island of Patmos. In a message that John was to deliver to a church in the city of Thyatira, Christ assured the faithful members that if they overcame the pitfalls they were facing, they would participate in the Messianic reign over the earth. Just as the Father had bestowed the anointed Son with authority to rule the nations, so the Son was now promising to share that power with his people. In other words, if they "kissed the Son" in obedience, they would share in the spoils when he returned (Rev. 2:25-27).

b. Psalm 110

Finally, the most significant Psalm that the NT uses to describe Jesus as Israel's Messiah and king is Psalm 110. It begins with the God of Israel (LORD) assuring his chosen king (Lord) that he will defeat all of his enemies. The Lord also promises this king that his rule will extend across the earth and that he will even fulfill a priestly role similar to that of the ancient character, Melchizedek.[79] For our purposes here, we want to give attention to the first verse only, because Jesus himself employs it during a conversation with some Pharisees and scribes (cf., Matt. 22:44; Mk. 12:36; Luke 20:42-43). During a litany of debates with these usual suspects, Jesus posed a question concerning the dual identity of "lords" in Psalm 110:1. Jesus asked the Jewish leaders whose son the Christ, or Messiah, will be. They easily retorted that he will be David's descendant and, at face value, this was not a wrong observation.

The twist, however, was that the Messianic story was bigger than they could see. This is why Jesus followed up with another question regarding Psalm 110:1. If the Christ was to be the son of David only, then why does David, as the author of the Psalm, refer to the Lord of Israel and another "Lord?" Though theoretically one might guess that he was referring to another king as a lord, no ruler ever experienced the promises described in the rest of the Psalm.[80] This is why Jesus pressed his opponents, because if the Messiah was merely another son, it made no sense for David to ascribe a higher status to him. Jesus was arguing that David was speaking prophetically of a figure that was distinct from the Lord but still greater than any human descendant. The Jewish leaders had no rebuttal to Jesus's point because they expected a human Messiah, not a divine one.[81]

READING THE PSALMS TODAY

We have shown some of the ways in which the Psalms contributed to Jesus's understanding of his identity as Israel's Messiah.[82] They provided prayers that he embraced, confessions of trust that he quoted, and theological truths that he defended. Cumulatively, they represented Israel's history of worship, which Jesus encapsulated in his own life. This is why we describe the Psalms as a diary or journal. They were accounts of past worshippers, especially David, who spoke out of the depths of their hearts about feelings that Jesus later shared and hopes that he would fulfill. Jesus was, then, the ultimate Psalmist, or perhaps even the pinnacle Psalm in human form as opposed to literary form.

In the end, then, we should be mindful that reading the Psalms today is a means of reflecting upon the prayers of God's people before us. Similar to the "hall of faith" in Hebrews 11, the Psalms remind us that our joy and our sadness are shared by believers of all generations. They do not happen in a vacuum. We are not the first people to pray to God, question his presence or motives for how he runs the world. What we do know is that in the end, just as God was always there for them, he will be there for us. Our God never leaves us—he left us a diary to remind us of that.

DISCUSSION

List a few truths you learned in this chapter that you'd not seen in Scripture before.

How do these truths apply to your life?

Why are these truths important to share with others?

9
JONAH

Anyone who grows up in North Texas has to get used to tornadoes. Every April or May, warning sirens can go off several times a week. And for those two months, it feels like we spend more time in our closets or bathtubs than anywhere else in our house. The duck-and-cover technique becomes the norm. Now, it would be nice to say we always pray and trust the Lord in those moments, but truthfully, we don't. We sometimes treat tornadoes like embodied deities, almost bowing down to them and begging them not to hit our house. "C'mon, tornado. Stay north of us. Don't come through here," we pray from our closets. We stop just short of leaving an offering on our doorstep.

Yet what would make matters even more disconcerting is if we really viewed a stormy twister that came our way as a direct act of judgment from the Lord. That would add a different element of stress entirely! Well, such a dramatic stage actually occurred in the life of an OT prophet named Jonah. As we shall see, not only did he experience a catastrophic event as an act of divine discipline, his story actually included events that pointed to the later life and ministry of Jesus himself.

JONAH'S GOD-GIVEN MISSION

Jonah's story begins much like others about God's prophets. The word, or message, of the Lord came to him with a commission to go preach. A key difference emerges in that he was a prophet of Israel who, in this case, was not sent to any part of Israel. Rather, he was summoned to preach against the great Assyrian city of Nineveh (which means "fish town"). Oddly enough, ancient new covenant folklore believed some type of fish-god founded the city.[83]

As the story goes, God tells Jonah that he must go preach to the Ninevites because "their evil has come up before me" (Jon. 1:1-2). The imagery here is interesting. Nineveh was so corrupt that the people's sin was like blaring music so loud that it was reaching up to the heavens. Such an account was standard protocol for many other stories about other OT prophets. When a nation was in sin and remained unrepentant, the Lord sent a prophet to confront the people. But like some prophets before him, Jonah expressed no desire to go. The only difference was that he didn't make excuses like, say, Moses, who thought his speech was insufficient; or Gideon who thought he was a nobody; or Jeremiah, who thought he was too young. No, instead Jonah did something unexpected. He packed his bags and fled from the Lord by going in the complete opposite direction. He traveled south to a seaport in Joppa in hopes of crossing the Mediterranean. So instead of going east to a region in modern-day Iraq, he left Israel and went west in hopes of reaching modern-day Spain!

Now at this point, a reader is naturally tempted to ask why in the world was Jonah so determined to avoid preaching in Nineveh. Was he afraid of being killed, rejected, or failure? It does not appear so, at least, not primarily. What we discover as the story unfolds is that Jonah simply lacked compassion for the Ninevites. The entire Assyrian nation was a feared enemy of Israel and other surrounding nations. Their reputation was horrid because of their pagan customs, open debauchery, and sadistic methods of warfare. In fact, it would only be a few decades in the future that Assyria could conquer the Northern Kingdom of Israel. Like any good Israelite, Jonah simply hated his country's bitter rival.

At the end of the story, we see that when the people heard Jonah's message of judgment, they repented. This outraged Jonah because he knew if they did humbly cast themselves before the Lord, he would forgive them. This meant that instead of getting what they "deserved," the Ninevites would receive the same kind of benevolent compassion that Israel often received. And whatever his deeper motivations were, what we do know is that Jonah wanted nothing to do with such an endeavor (cf., Jon. 3:10-4:1-3). Thus, when we read the whole story, essentially Jonah ran because he would rather defy the Lord's commission than see a people be restored. How's that for a loving prophet?

JONAH IS DISCIPLINED BY THE LORD

In his trip across the Great Sea, Jonah failed to remember that when God commissioned someone to be a prophet or fulfill a prophetic task, he rarely, if ever, took "no" for an answer. He sent Aaron to accompany Moses because of his reluctance. He empowered the timid Gideon to serve a military judge for Israel against the rivaling Midianites. And he rebuked Jeremiah's excuse about his youth by reminding him that he was called to be a prophet while he was in his mother's womb. This kind of consistency was not going to change simply because Jonah's excuses were different—Jonah would not receive an excused absence from the mantle of God's call. He thought he could run away from the Lord's commands by putting as many miles between himself and Nineveh as possible. The only problem is that the Lord's presence was not restricted one place on a map. He was present in Nineveh so he could know their sinfulness. He was in Israel so he knew where Jonah lived. And he was present both on the seas and in Tarshish so he was already waiting in the places where Jonah was trying to hide.

Jonah's situation then takes a turn for the worst in the most well-known part of the story. Scripture says that the Lord sent a strong wind over the sea that led to a storm that threatened the wellbeing of everyone on board. This set the stage for Jonah to learn about the price of disobedience.

1. Sea Gods, Sailors, and Storms

The storm caused quite a bit of alarm among the sailors aboard. It is possible that these sailors believed in an ancient new covenant tale about Yam, the god of sea and chaos. Yam was a volatile, uncontrollable being. Another deity named Ba'al, sometimes regarded as Yam's brother, was considered a friend to sailors. But he was unable to control Yam. He could only contain him at times. When water rushed upon the shore and was sent backwards, Ba'al was keeping Yam in check. Naturally then, even Ba'al's help did not prevent sailors from fearing Yam's wrath. This was especially true out on the open sea because they felt like no one could help them.

This mythology provides a potential clue to understanding the cultural context for this part of Jonah's story. So, when the account says that "the Lord threw a great wind onto the sea, and such a great storm arose on the sea that the ship threatened to break apart" (Jon. 1:4), the Hebrew word for "sea" is none other than *yam*. If they were familiar with the old seafaring folklore, these sailors might have thought the sea god just woke up prematurely from his afternoon nap. But at the very least, they all saw the overwhelming waves threatening their boat. They called out to their gods for help to no avail. They began throwing cargo overboard in hopes of lightening the weight of the ship. And amidst this frantic activity, they discovered Jonah—who was curiously sleeping through the storm—and woke him up to see if his God could come to their rescue.

2. Jonah and the Great Fish

Jonah approached the deck of the ship to see all the sailors clamoring to cast lots, hoping to find out that this sudden storm was the result of someone who had ticked off a certain god. Most likely, these sailors believed in all kinds of deities. No doubt they were conjuring all kinds of notions about who had done what to whom. Yet as Proverbs 16:33 says, lots can be cast arbitrarily, but the outcomes are ultimately under the Lord's control. What were the odds that pagan sailors who were enslaved to all kinds of superstitions and pagan practices could cast lots that would fall on Jonah? Well, if the Lord was involved, pretty good. And to add to the irony, Jonah had gone to such great lengths to escape the Lord's presence, and all it took was a sailors' gambling ritual to catch him.

The sailors demanded to know what Jonah's story was. Knowing that the cat was out of the bag, he let them know that he was a Hebrew who served the one true God, maker of heaven, earth, and the seas. They could not believe Jonah would try to flee from his God—such an act could jeopardize the lives of those around him. And their fears were becoming reality. Now at this point, we are not sure whether Jonah felt pity for the sailors or preferred to die instead of going to Nineveh. What we do know is that he told the sailors to throw him overboard so that the storm would calm. The sailors were glad to oblige. They even prayed to Jonah's God in hopes that they could avoid the wrath of the crashing waves. Basically, they asked God to prevent them from being collateral damage for Jonah's sin. Amazingly, after they threw him overboard, the storm ceased. This left such an impression on the sailors that they took oaths and offered a sacrifice in gratitude. Thus, even Jonah's rebellion was used by God as a testimony to people outside the confines of Israel.

The story then mentions one of the most bizarre ways in which the Lord got the attention of a disobedient servant. The Scripture says that the Lord appointed a great fish (a whale *perhaps*), to swallow Jonah. As we know, he was stuck in this plight for three days and nights. At this time creatures who lived in the sea were often viewed as mysterious and powerful because they lurked in the territory that man could not conquer. If the Lord controlled the land, the winds, and living things in the oceans, then in the minds of the ancients, he was sovereign over all creation. Not surprisingly, we are told that such a traumatic experience humbled Jonah to the point of prayer. He petitioned the Lord while in the belly of the fish, asking to be delivered. He confessed that salvation only came from the Lord, whether it be for him in a great fish or, dare he admit it, for the Ninevites if they were to repent. The Lord graciously answered by allowing the whale to have indigestion and hurl Jonah back onto the shores. Whether Jonah actually died in the whale and was resuscitated or not, we do not know. What's for certain is that he was as good as dead until God chose to spare him. And as we shall see, this same kind of scenario was replicated in Jesus's life as well.

JONAH REPENTS, PREACHES, AND COMPLAINS

One of the most beautiful passages in the OT occurs at this point in Jonah's story. After he life was spared, the Bible says that the word of the Lord came to Jonah a second time. He was given another chance to do the right thing—the perfect image of redemption. Jonah is told once more to go preach to the Ninevites, and indeed he does. The city was so massive that it would take three days to walk through it. But on his first day of preaching that God's judgment would come in forty days, the people began to repent in hopes that they would be spared. Word even reached the king about the matter. He was so moved that he decreed a citywide prayer vigil in the hopes that Jonah's God would relent on his forty-day countdown. And just as God spared the sailors from the storm and delivered Jonah from the great fish, once again he showed himself to be merciful by forgiving the Ninevites.

Though this is beginning to sound like the happy ending of a summer blockbuster, the book is not over—Jonah's story contains one extra twist. Thus far, we were surprised to see Jonah fleeing from the Lord when he was summoned. Yet not to be outdone, the Lord's way of tracking Jonah down and giving him incentive to do the right thing was quite shocking, too. Then, another curveball is thrown when we read about the Ninevites actually *repenting* after hearing Jonah's message. After all of this, Jonah becomes angry because the Lord did exactly what he thought he would do—forgive the repenting Ninevites (Jonah 4:1-3). Notice that in his sermon, Jonah left out the possibility that they could escape God's wrath. He had no interest in giving them an out.

Jonah's demeanor here is quite disturbing. He tells God that he intentionally tried to delay his mission by fleeing to Tarshish. He becomes so melodramatic that he even asks the Lord to take his life. Initially, he asked the Lord to spare his life because he was terrified in the bowels of a whale, and rightfully so. Now, he's so depressed over the Ninevites' repentance that he would rather die than see them live. Amidst Jonah's pity party, the Lord then allowed a plant to grow over him while he sulked in the middle-eastern sun. Jonah was grateful for the shade. During the night, though, the Lord sent a worm to eat away at the plant until it withered away by the next morning. Then instead of causing another storm, the Lord sent a scorching wind that made the morning sun all the more unrelenting. Jonah, in true form, became even angrier. And it is this point that the Book of Jonah comes to an end. Jonah went into an emotional tailspin because he thought the Lord was adding insult to injury. Not only were the wicked Ninevites off the hook because they repented, but now Jonah had to watch the city from afar with no shade or protection from the elements.

The story concludes with God rebuking Jonah's warped reasoning. How could he be so upset about losing a plant that he did not cultivate? How could he not understand that the Lord would choose to be compassionate on thousands of people that he had created? We never truly see the end of Jonah's story. We only know that it ends with God attempting to reason with Jonah's hard heart.

JESUS AND JONAH AS PROPHETS OF ISRAEL

At first glance, one might wonder what Jonah has in common with Jesus. His bad attitudes, rebellious antics, and the wild way in which the Lord got his attention seem to be a far cry from anything that Jesus went through. We might be tempted to only highlight the geographical region they held in common. We read in 2 Kings 14:25, for instance, that Jonah was from a place called Gathhepher—a place possibly located just three miles northeast of Nazareth, thereby making Jonah and Jesus both prophets of Galilee.[84] But when we begin reading the Gospels and the rest of the NT, there are several important parallels that are made between elements of Jonah's story and the life that Christ lived.

First, we see the contrast between Jonah's attitude as a reluctant, and even prejudiced, prophet and Christ's willingness to follow the will of his Father. Jonah was a prophet who reluctantly obeyed the Lord because preaching to Nineveh was preferable to the inner anatomy of a whale. Jesus, on the other hand, was given a mission that was national and even international. In one sense, he was sent to the people of Israel because it was to this nation that the Messianic promises were originally given. Jesus's entire life, except for his brief stay in Egypt during his infancy, was spent in Israel. He was born in the Bethlehem, the city of David; he ministered in both major regions of first century Israel, Galilee and Judea; and he died and was resurrected in the capitol city of Jerusalem.

Second, we see that Jesus extended his message beyond Israel. He interacted with Samaritans, residents of the Gentile cities of Tyre and Sidon, and even commended the faith of a Roman centurion. In turn, he reached out to the Gentiles because Israel's redemption entailed the promise that other nations also would be blessed. This is exactly what Jonah wanted to ignore. He wanted nothing to do with the Ninevites receiving the same kind of mercy that Israel experienced. Because Jesus came to redeem Israel and the nations, essentially his mission was global in nature. We find this language in John's Gospel especially where we read that Jesus became the Lamb of God who would take away the sins not only of Israel, but of the world (the nations) (John 1:29). Also, in John 3:16-17, we see that the Father loved the world that he gave his Son so that all (Jew or Gentile) who believe might have death-defeating life in the kingdom age to come (eternal life).

What we have here is a huge contrast between two of Israel's prophets. Jonah was given a message of repentance that he was to deliver to a Gentile city so they could have an opportunity to repent and be spared God's judgment. Similarly, Christ was God's Word in human form who was sent to preach the consummate message of the kingdom of heaven so that both Jews and Gentiles could escape the ultimate judgment upon sin in the age to come. Jonah wanted nothing to do with seeing his God, the Lord of Israel, grant forgiveness to a pagan nation. Christ, on the other hand, chose to leave heaven and come to earth knowing that he would not receive the same kind of response that Jonah witnessed in Nineveh. He knew that he would come to Israel as her consummate prophet only to be rejected by her (Matt. 27:21-23; cf., Isa. 53:3).

Still, Jesus looked at the needs of others over his own and, as Hebrews says, endured the cross because of the joy and glory that was set before him (Heb. 12:1-2). He was willing to be slain because he could bring glory to his Father by providing a means of forgiving individuals from all nations, so they could one day have solidarity together as his redeemed people (Rev. 7:11-12). Jonah's nightmare was Jesus's goal.

JESUS, JONAH, AND STORMS

Another set of parallels lies in the fact that both Jonah and Jesus were caught sleeping on a boat in a storm. All three of the Synoptic Gospels mention this account (see Matt. 8:23-27; Mk. 4:35-41; Lk. 8:22-25). We read that Jesus wanted to cross the Sea of Galilee after ministering to some crowds. As their journey began, Jesus took some type of pillow to grab some shuteye at the boat's stern. Most likely, he was tired from extensive teaching and ministering to the people's needs.[85] It is interesting that Jonah was asleep while trying to hide from the Lord, while Jesus was resting because he was physically spent from serving his Father.

Then suddenly, Jesus's excursion harkens back to Jonah's story because a storm came upon the waters, so much so that the waves were coming into the boat filling it with water. But Jesus was still asleep, either because he was a heavy sleeper or more likely because, again, he was exhausted. The situation was becoming so dire that like the frightened sailors on the boat with Jonah, Jesus's disciples were panicking. They quickly awakened Jesus, asking him if he realized that they were about to be a first-century version of the Titanic. Jesus initially gets up and is surprised by their lack of faith. All of the miracles they had seen him perform, plus the fact that he himself was not worried about the storm, were not enough to assure them that they were safe. To their credit, though, they knew at some level that Jesus had the power to help them, which is more than we can say for Jonah. He knew God was sovereign, but also knew that he was on a boat because he was defying God's call. So, he jumped overboard rather than facing the God he was running from. He took his chances in the open sea rather than turning his eyes to the heavens. The disciples chose otherwise—they ran straight to their Master.[86]

From here, Jesus stood in the boat to do something unthinkable. He did not have the disciples cast lots or perform any other kind of random ceremony to figure out the purpose of the storm. Rather, he exercised the same kind of authority that God did in Jonah's story. The Lord of Israel sent a storm Jonah's way, appointed a great fish in the sea to swallow him after he was thrown overboard, and sent Jonah a small plant to provide a parabolic moment that confronted him about his rotten attitude; Jesus, similarly, now showed the same kind of power by speaking to the storm; in essence, he told the storm to be quiet. No one had to jump overboard. No customs had to be enacted. Instead, Jesus exercised the same divine authority over creation as his Father. The Gospels say that the winds ceased and there was a great calm. Just as God brought tranquility to the sea when Jonah's disobedience was addressed, the elements obeyed Jesus at his word. Then, after admonishing the storm, he turned his attention to his disciples to admonish them. Since the storm had ceased, it was time to address the storm that was still in the hearts of his disciples.

Undoubtedly, the disciples were so stunned at this point that it took a while for all of this to soak in. However they processed this event later, one thing was obvious—the disciples now had all kinds of new questions about who Jesus really was. They began asking themselves what kind of man Jesus expressed the same kind of power that the God of Israel exhibited throughout OT, including stories like Jonah's.

JESUS, JONAH, AND DELIVERANCE FROM DEATH

The final connection we can see between these two figures is an explicit link that the NT makes between Jonah's story. Most notably, we see comparisons in the audiences that Jesus often addressed, and his final death and resurrection. What is most noteworthy about these connections is that in the Gospels, the only prophet with whom Jesus directly compares himself is, in fact, Jonah. He quotes from numerous OT prophets, alludes to many of their ideas, and uses much of their literary imagery when he preached to various crowds—yet Jonah is the only one that he explicitly identifies with. We see these parallels in three particular texts: two occur in Matthew, where Jesus discusses the matter in 12:38-42 and briefly mentions the point again in passing in 16:1-4; the other instance is found in Luke 11:29-32, where an extra bit of information is added that Matthew omits.

One of the most important themes in the Gospels is authority. When Jesus taught or performed miracles, people could not deny his extraordinary way with words, nor would they question the influence he had over sicknesses, death, or demons. But in order to exhibit such feats, one had to have a source from which they were deriving such abilities. And that is why Jesus's audience was constantly wondering by what authority was he able to do all of these things. If only the God of Israel could forgive sins, rule over nature, or give life to the dead, then who was this Jesus who claimed to be able to do all of these things? And by what authority could Jesus do these things? This was a million-dollar question in the Gospel accounts.

Jesus was clearly aware that such a concern was legitimate. He knew that false prophets could perform miracles and potentially deceive the masses—that is why he decided to up the ante with various supernatural acts. But they were always to benefit people, confront the sinfulness of the nation, or humiliate the satanic forces of darkness. He expressed his heavenly authority in ways that revealed divine compassion and righteousness for God's kingdom, not man's. They were signs of his true authority from his Father as the Son of Man who had come to represent a kingdom not of this world. The problem is that not everyone was interested in discovering if his authority was authentic, because if it were, that would mean they must submit to it.

1. The Sign of Jonah and the Sign of the Son of Man: Matthew 12:38-42

In his first reference to Jonah, Jesus tells some religious leaders asking for more "signs" that they are an "evil and adulterous generation," because only those kinds of people constantly demand signs, especially when God's messenger has already provided an ample amount of them. This phrase harkens back to the people of Noah's day who heard his faithful preaching for years and refused to listen (Gen. 7:1). It also is used of the generation of Israelites who failed to enter the Promised Land because of their unbelief (Deut. 1:35). They witnessed all the "signs" in the ten plagues of Egypt, the parting of the Red Sea, and his glorious appearance at Mount Sinai. Yet they were unsure as to whether the Lord could give them victory over the rivaling tribes in Canaan. Jesus is making the same point here. These religious leaders had heard about the things he was doing and even witnessed some of them firsthand. Now they want more?

Even though they were manipulative and corrupt, Jesus gives them one more sign—one provided by the prophet Jonah. He then makes a cryptic parallel with Jonah, who found himself in the belly of the great fish for three days and three nights. In the same way, Jesus says, the Son of Man who will be in the heart of the earth for three days and three nights. Of course, this sign does not help much in the moment—his audience is totally unaware that he will soon be crucified, buried, and raised from the dead three days later. Jesus's comments here are similar to those that we find in John 2:19, where he says that if Jewish leaders destroyed the sanctuary, he would rebuild it in three days. This baffled them because they knew it took decades to build Herod's temple. However, they did not interpret Jesus correctly, because he was speaking about his body, the new dwelling of God's presence (Jn. 2:20-21). Similarly, the same kind of dissonance is occurring in Matthew's account here. Jesus shot over their heads, but only because he wanted his prediction to hit home once the resurrection occurred. And when it did, Jesus knew he would be vindicated and his authority will be upheld.

He also says that once the sign of Jonah was complete, their sinful hearts would be exposed. In fact, the Ninevites would indict them, because they heard the message of Jonah and believed. He also alludes to the OT story where the Queen of Sheba came to hear the wisdom of Solomon. Her acts of faith, which were based only on hearsay about Solomon's greatness, would condemn the religious leaders because one stood before them who was far greater than Solomon. Jesus showed little tolerance for requests for signs because such demands were standard behavior for people of evil and wicked generations. They wanted to see a show, not the power of God.

Nevertheless, the sign that Jesus mentioned was clear: Jonah was swallowed up by a great fish and faced inevitable death. But he prayed to the Lord to be delivered so he could accomplish the task he was originally called to do. Likewise, Israel's ultimate prophet would enter the pit of death and be cursed as a transgressor on behalf of sinners. Yet, his Father would vindicate him by raising him from the dead. This would be the ultimate sign for this unbelieving generation.[87]

2. The Sign of Jonah as a Sign to Israel: Luke 11:29-32

Luke's account of Jesus's discussion about Jonah includes many of the same points that Matthew mentions. He records Jesus's accusation that his Jewish opponents were part of an evil, perverse generation because they were entrenched in unbelief as evidenced by their demands for signs. He also retains Jesus's claims that the faith expressed by the Queen of the South and the Ninevites would indict his stubborn listeners because he was greater than both Solomon and Jonah. Luke adds one feature, though, that deserves a little bit of attention.

In Luke's account, Jesus said that as the Son of Man, he would serve as a sign to his audience, just as Jonah was a sign to the Ninevites. But how was this the case? How was Jonah's experience in the belly of the great fish, which again is what Matthew appears to identify as the point of reference, possibly a sign to his Assyrian counterparts? Most likely, what Luke is emphasizing is that while the great fish incident was indeed important, the true comparison was that both Jesus and Jonah preached a message of restoration to a people facing judgment.[88] The only difference was that Jonah's audience repented, whereas many in Jesus's day did not. Therefore, just as Jonah's presence to proclaim God's word among the Gentiles served as a sign that divine judgment was on the horizon, Jesus's presence among the Jews was a sign that they needed to repent as well.

When we combine the claims that Jesus made about Jonah in both Matthew and Luke, we discover two fascinating elements about our Savior. One is that Jonah's encounter with the great fish served as a prelude to Jesus's later experience of death itself. We see this in Jesus's claim that Jonah's descent into the fish's belly (where he may have possibly died) corresponded to his upcoming descent into the grave. Likewise, just as Jonah was coughed up by the fish onto the coast so he could go preach to the Ninevites, Jesus would later be raised from the dead as a vindication of his identity as the Savior for all who believe—whether they be Jewish, Assyrian, or any other race. Relatedly, the other factor between Jonah and Jesus is that Jonah's post-fish presence among the Ninevites was a sign that God's judgment was coming if they refused to repent. In like manner, Jesus's presence among the nation of Israel was a sign that salvation could be received if one believed, but judgment would be incurred by anyone who rejected his message.

SAFE FROM THE STORMS

No ominous Texas tornado ever hit our house, though a few times they came close. In any case, we always expressed gratitude to the Lord only for his protection. And by doing so, we are reliving similar events that Jonah, the disciples, and even Jesus himself experienced. We entrust ourselves to our Father's will and power. Jonah did when he asked God for help in the depths of the ocean. The disciples did when they thought a storm was going to envelop them. And Jesus did when he gave himself to his Father's will, even if it meant death on a cross.

Because of this simple truth, we should avoid the natural temptation to emulate the example of the sailors in Jonah's day, thinking the storm was somehow controlled by other divine powers. We should also beware of the idea that natural forces are just random acts that occur arbitrarily when the right elements converge. Instead, we should cast ourselves on God's provision because when we do, Christ will give us the same kind of peace that he gave his disciples.

The reason we can have this confidence is because no matter what kind of storm comes our way, whether it be literal or not, God does not ignore our cries for help. He answered Jonah when he prayed for deliverance even though the reason he was in trouble was because of his own disobedience. Jesus also did not dismiss his disciples when they were distraught from threatening rain and crashing waves. Instead he silenced the storm by telling it to be quiet. And our heavenly Father did not leave our Lord abandoned in the grave. He raised him in glory as the conqueror of death and the prototype for a new creation. In fact, because of his victory, Revelation 21-22 describes a new earth that is to come where there will be no sea, no unchartered territory, no chaos, no place where nature can overtake our lives. Since we serve such a Savior, may we never be like those in Jesus's generation who refused to repent. May we never neglect a greater message than the people of Nineveh could have ever imagined.[89]

DISCUSSION

List a few truths you learned in this chapter that you'd not seen in Scripture before.

How do these truths apply to your life?

Why are these truths important to share with others?

RETURNING TO EMMAUS

Coming full circle, we travel one more time to that ancient road to Emmaus where Jesus talked with two disciples about the Law and the prophets. We discussed how all of their doubts, fears, confusion, and questions were based upon their inability to reconcile their understanding of what the OT said about the Messiah with what had happened to Jesus. Yet all of this foggy confusion dissipated once Israel's Messiah slowly open their eyes to what the OT truly taught. And once their perspective was realigned so they could see how Christ's death and resurrection were central to the OT hopes, they were never the same.

That moment of realization, that "ah-ha moment" which those disciples experienced, is precisely what we want to replicate in some small way. Obviously, hearing the master teacher, Jesus himself, would be the ultimate experience to have. But the NT is full of examples of how he interpreted the OT, and the early Church followed his lead in their readings of it. Therefore, what would thrill our hearts as authors is if readers could see the connections that these nine chapters have made between parts of the OT and Jesus, so that their hearts can be emboldened to study God's Word even more. Then, we could all echo the sentiment of those early disciples by feeling our own hearts burn with hope because we can see how Scripture still speaks of him.

JESUS WASN'T AFRAID OF HIS OT

When talking about the OT's relationship with Jesus and the NT, some would say that this book is a waste of time. They would say that "the God of the OT" seems angry and judgmental, and we have no business talking about him in conjunction with the forgiving, kind Jesus of the NT. But this is wrongheaded because, as we've seen, Jesus and the NT writers rely heavily on the OT to stake their claim about God and how he will save mankind. Let's discuss this further.

In Volume 1 of *Reformed Dogmatics*, Herman Bavinck lists out four ways that Jesus, the apostles, and other New Testament writers showed clear reverence for the authority of the OT, particularly as a divinely-authored text. Immediately prior to this section, he also convincingly demonstrates why OT authors, prophets, and other writers considered their message *the very words of God himself*. Jesus and the NT writers, then, carry this view of Scripture's authority into their own message, seeing their own words as God's Word (Jn. 1:1; 2 Pet. 1:20-21; 3:15-16). Here is Bavinck's list, summarized and edited for clarity:

1. "The formula with which the OT is cited in the NT varies, but it always shows that to the writers of the NT the OT is of divine origin and bears divine authority. ... This manner of citation clearly and distinctly teaches us that to Jesus and the apostles the Scripture of the old covenant, though composed of various parts and traceable to different authors, actually formed one organic whole whose author was God himself."
2. "Several times Jesus and the apostles also definitely affirmed and taught the divine authority of OT Scripture. Scripture is a unified

whole, which can neither be broken up and destroyed as a totality or in its parts." This is key to understand, because Jesus and the NT authors, at the time of their speaking and writing, only considered the OT as their authoritative set of texts.

3. "Jesus and the apostles never take a critical position toward the content of the OT but accept it totally and without reservation. They unconditionally accept the Scripture of the OT as true and divine in all its parts, not only in its religious-ethical pronouncements or in the passages in which God himself speaks, but also in its historical components."

4. "Dogmatically, to Jesus and the apostles the OT is the foundation of doctrine, the source of solutions, and the end of all argument. ... And, to their mind, this divine authority of Scripture extended so far that a single word, even an iota or a dot, is covered by it." Jesus was clear about this when he told his disciples on the road to Emmaus to look back at the OT for the answers to their questions about the Messiah's life and ministry.[90]

It's become somewhat of a trend recently to claim that we need to rescue Jesus and the NT from the megalomaniac, genocidal God of the OT. That OT God can't *really* be what God is like because, well, Jesus isn't like that. (And Jesus *is* God, after all.) Evangelicals, then, need to get *Jesus* right before they worry about getting the *Bible* right. They say that "to understand Jesus" means, at least in part, to understand that "love your enemies" (Matt. 5:44) is at odds with "show them no mercy" (Deut. 7:2).

Christian scholars, pastors, and laypeople alike are picking up this dry, stale bread in hopes of selling it to the public as a buttered loaf straight from the oven. But people know stale bread when they taste it. And they should rightly spit it out.

There is no life in an OT divorced from the NT. This oft-cited quote from Paul to Timothy is not merely a Sunday school lesson in Bible-rule-following—it's a proclamation about the authority of the OT:

> *All Scripture is inspired by God and is profitable for teaching, for rebuking, for correcting, for training in righteousness, so that the man of God may be complete, equipped for every good work. (2 Tim. 3:16-17)*

Paul isn't saying, "Scripture is a good road map for life, so don't worry about the weird stuff." Paul is saying, "Scripture (in this case, the OT) is God's breath—his Word—and therefore life-giving."

The community of faith—where this teach-rebuke-correct-training quadrilateral takes place—is built around the Scriptures. There's no need to hide from it. It won't hurt you. God breathed into Adam's nostrils and he came to life; God breathed into the Scriptures and we come to life.

This is not to say that we have to be "literalists" or "closed-minded." The Bible isn't immune to varying genres, turns-of-phrase, storytelling, hyperbole, round numbers, hard statements, and the like. This book has shown us that. It's a book from its time, but it's not a book stuck in time. So we don't have to turn a blind eye to "problem passages" or deep questions. Our heads can stay well above the sand.

But we should, along with those considerations, take the Bible on its terms and seek answers on its terms. We too quickly want to ditch its claims in favor of the latest scientific trends, an emotional preference, or to create palatable teaching, when some of the most difficult passages (like God kicking Adam and Eve out of the Garden over a piece of fruit, or

God freeing the Israelites from the Egyptians via river-drowning) inaugurate some of the most redemptive themes in Scripture.

THE OLD TESTAMENT ACCORDING TO JESUS

Christians should specifically take the OT on Jesus's terms. After all, he claims that it's about him on more than one occasion, and NT writers claim he embodies its message. He spoke of the OT as though it was fully trustworthy. He was comfortable suggesting that "the word of God cannot be broken" (Jn. 10:35), and perhaps his most powerful and consistent indictment on opponents and doubters was, "Haven't you read the Scriptures?" (Matt. 19:4; et al.).

Sure, he employed some surprising hermeneutics. He and the NT writers interpret OT passages and stories in ways that make us scratch our heads. We saw some of this in the chapters of this book. But it's one thing to say they made surprising pots out of OT clay; it's quite another to say they were disposing of the OT altogether. We shouldn't think that Jesus sticks the OT under a rug like a bad coffee stain. No, he sets it front and center without apology.

For example, in Matthew 10:15 we see Jesus (the *love-your-enemies* Jesus) cite a horrific moment in OT—God's destructive judgment of Sodom and Gomorrah (Gen. 19). First, Jesus affirms that God's destruction of Sodom and Gomorrah really happened. Second, he warned his audience that the judgment they receive could be worse for them than Sodom and Gomorrah's judgment. Not only did he not qualify himself or apologize for God's judgment of sin, but he clearly felt no need to.

Denying, explaining away, or ignoring the OT causes more questions than answers. Here are a few questions we must answer if we separate the OT and NT from one another:

- How can we trust the NT if we can't trust its foundation, the OT?
- How can the reader "get Jesus right" without understanding the OT, which he says is about him?
- How can we trust Jesus himself to be a truth-teller if we think the OT has nothing to do with him—despite the fact that he relies on its claims to justify his own life and ministry?
- How can we preach about the forgiveness, mercy, and justice of God if he's not allowed to judge those who defy his plans or oppress victims?
- How can we know that our sins have truly been forgiven by Jesus if we ignore the OT's original report that we need a substitute for our sins?

These questions remind us that the way Jesus speaks of the OT throughout the Bible is crucial to Christian living. We can't understand the Bible with the OT, and we can't trust Jesus without it. Hopefully we've shown this to be true in the chapters of this book.

HUNGER FOR MORE

We would like to thank readers for taking this journey with us. Our goal has been to capture briefly some of the ways in which the OT forms a beautiful mosaic of Jesus our Savior. And we endeavored to demonstrate this by expounding on select OT characters and themes. We looked at how the lives of Adam, Noah, Melchizedek, Moses, David, and Jonah prefigure the life and ministry of the Christ. Likewise, we traced how the stories of the Temple, the Psalms, and the people of Israel unfold so readers could see how their functions found their ultimate fulfillment in Jesus himself.

We must admit, though, that this list only scratches the surface. There are all sorts of people, events, and prophecies that contribute to the grand hall of OT hopes that anticipate the coming of Christ. In fact, there are over 300 prophecies about the Messiah in the OT. There are numerous NT references to the OT in relation to Jesus that we did not explore here. We could add a host of other chapters that deal with figures such as Joseph, Joshua, Isaiah's suffering servant, and Hosea. Or we could even dig into the vast well of these fascinating prophecies that the OT provides about who the Messiah would be and what he would do for his people. Indeed, this book could serve as an opening volume in an entire series.

Nevertheless, we still hope our brief tour can make at least two impressions. First, we want readers to rekindle an old, or perhaps discover a new, passion for Scripture because of how it speaks about the coming Messiah in so many captivating ways. We have seen that there is not just one way in which characters, topics, or prophecies describe who the Messiah would be. Rather, there was no way a single approach could ever be enough. Jesus's identity as the Son of God and his work as our Savior have so many nuances of meaning that the OT had to compact a multitude of features into one huge narrative so it could give us a fully-orbed portrait. It included the lives of people, symbols, poetic Psalms, prophecies, and many other factors so future readers could look back and see how the Lord provided a wealth of information regarding the future Redeemer.

The other impact we want this book to have is simply to whet every reader's appetite for more. We want you to hunger for more of God's

Word—a story that points again and again to the God-man, Jesus Christ. No greater achievement could we enjoy than for these nine chapters to serve as a launching pad upon which readers can be propelled to further study of Scripture. And in turn, one's deeper love for Scripture would result in a stronger devotion to Christ.

RECOMMENDED READING

Alexander, T. Desmond. *From Eden to New Jerusalem: An Introduction to Biblical Theology*. Grand Rapids, MI: Kregel, 2008.

Bartholomew, Craig G. and Michael W. Goheen. *The Drama of Scripture: Finding Our Place in the Biblical Story*. Grand Rapids, MI: Baker Academic, 2014.

Bird, Michael F. *Jesus Is the Christ: The Messianic Testimony of the Gospels*. Downers Grove, IL: InterVarsity, 2012.

Clowney, Edmund P. *The Unfolding Mystery: Discovering Christ in the Old Testament*. Phillipsburg, NJ: P&R Publishing, 2013.

Goldsworthy, Graeme. *According to the Plan: The Unfolding Revelation of God in the Bible*. Downers Grove: InterVarsity, 1991.

Guthrie, Nancy. *The One Year Book of Discovering Jesus in the Old Testament*. Carol Stream, IL: Tyndale House, 2010.

Medders, J. A. and Brandon D. Smith. *Rooted: Theology for Growing Christians*. (n.p.): Rainer Publishing, 2016.

Murray, David. *Jesus on Every Page: 10 Simple Ways to Seek and Find Christ in the Old Testament*. Nashville: Thomas Nelson, 2013.

Roberts, Vaughan. *God's Big Picture: Tracing the Storyline of the Bible*. Downers Grove, IL: InterVarsity, 2002.

Schreiner, Thomas R. *The King in His Beauty: A Biblical Theology of the Old and New Testaments*. Grand Rapids, MI: Baker, 2013.

Wright, Christopher J. H. *Knowing Jesus Through the Old Testament*. Downers Grove, IL: InterVarsity, 2014.

ENDNOTES

1. There are many longstanding debates pertaining to further details about what it means for humanity to be created in God's *image* and *likeness*. However, we cannot pursue any of them here because they go beyond the scope of this book. For those who might be interested in learning more about the subject, we recommend that one consult Anthony A. Hoekema, *Created in God's Image* (Grand Rapids, MI: Eerdmans Publishing Co., 1986) and J. Richard Middleton, *The Liberating Image: The Imago Dei in Genesis 1* (Grand Rapids, MI: Brazo Press, 2005).
2. Thomas R. Schreiner, *The King in His Beauty: A Biblical Theology of the Old and NTs* (Grand Rapids, MI: Baker, 2013), 6.
3. This title does not necessarily intend to describe anything intrinsic to the tree itself as if its fruit contained some sort of supernatural ingredient that made one good or evil. Rather, most likely it is that this specific tree is designated by God as off limits thereby creating a moral context in which evil could be a possibility.
4. Some speculate that the language used here in Genesis to describe God's commands to Adam and Eve is intrinsically covenantal in nature. The reason being that there is instruction on what they are to do and a clear warning of judgment if they violate the one prohibition. The

deduction is that possibly the divine intent was to place Adam and Eve on an initial probationary period of testing to see if they would obey God's commands. And if they did, they would be permitted to eat of the tree of life and be confirmed in their innocent state. Though this is to some extent conjecture, it does seem to make some sense of the narrative.

5 As Bill Watson, Assistant Professor of Greek and NT at Criswell College, says: "She allows herself to be deceived into thinking that she could grasp after that which is already hers, and in doing so ironically loses the very thing she possesses already."

6 T. Desmond Alexander, *From Eden to New Jerusalem: An Introduction to Biblical Theology* (Grand Rapids, MI: Kregel, 2008), 79.

7 Ibid., 101.

8 Jared C. Wilson, *The Wonder-Working God: Seeing the Glory of Jesus in His Parables* (Wheaton, IL: Crossway, 2014), 31.

9 Though we do not intend to get bogged down in the theological technicalities of Christology here, the point is that the person of Jesus was first the co-eternal and co-equal Son of the Father. Then at a point in history, the Son took upon himself a distinct human nature, thereby becoming a man, Jesus the Christ.

10 Kevin J. Vanhoozer, *Faith Speaking Understanding: Performing the Drama of Doctrine* (Louisville, KY: Westminster John Knox Press, 2014), 86.

11 Christopher J. H. Wright, *Knowing Jesus through the OT* (Downers Grove, IL: IVP Academic, 1992), 177.

12 Craig G. Bartholomew and Michael W. Goheen, *The Drama of Scripture: Finding Our Place in the Biblical Story* (Grand Rapids, MI: Baker Academic, 2004), 208.

13 Vanhoozer, *Faith Speaking Understanding*, 30.
14 R. S. Hess, "Noah," in the *New Dictionary of Biblical Theology*, eds., T. Desmond Alexander, et al. (Downers Grove: Intervarsity, 2000), 678.
15 Ibid. 678-79.
16 An excellent discussion of these points can be found in helpful survey by Daniel Streett, "As it was in the Days of Noah: The Prophets' Typological Interpretation of Noah's Flood," *Criswell Theological Review* 5, no. 1 (Fall 2007), 33-51.
17 Hess, "Noah," 679.
18 Since the word "angel" simply means "messenger," there is some debate as to whether or not this angel is Christ himself, or one of God's heavenly angels.
19 Matt Carter and Halim Suh, "The Creator Destroys and Redeems," in *The Gospel Project Bible* (Nashville, TN: Holman Bible Publishers, 2016), 11.
20 S. J. Andrews, "Melchizedek," in the *Dictionary of the OT Pentateuch*, eds., T. Desmond Alexander and David W. Baker (Downers Grove: Intervarsity, 2003), 563.
21 There are several other options, but you get the idea.
22 Ibid. Andrews also points other passages with similar uses of both words that refer to the Lord in Jeremiah 38:6, Haggai 1:1 and Ezra 3:2.
23 Ibid.
24 This is not to say that occasionally a king could not perform priest-like actions or that priests could not offer leadership for the people. But in no instance did kings serve as official priests or vice-versa. In fact, as we shall see, OT regulations were such that no one could meet both sets of criteria.
25 Other sources confirm this connection such as the Dead Sea Scrolls

and Josephus. See Ibid.; and D. G. Peterson, "Melchizedek," in the *New Dictionary of Biblical Theology*, eds., T. Desmond Alexander, et al. (Downers Grove: Intervarsity, 2000), 659.

26 More than likely, Sodom and Gommorah were vassal cities that paid "protection money" or tribute to Chedorlaomer. But again, the details are not mentioned.

27 Interestingly enough, it is here where Abraham (Abram) is first called a "Hebrew" (Gen. 14:13). It should also be mentioned that Abraham was obligated tribally to rescue Lot because he was the patriarch relative. His position as the head father of the various families created an expectation that he would use his resources to help any family members in need. See a great discussion of this point in Sandra Richter, The Epic of Eden (Downer Grove: Intervarsity, 2008), 43.

28 Andrews, "Melchizedek,"564.

29 The way in which this Psalm refers to the Messiah is discussed in a bit more detail in Chapter 8.

30 R. T. France, *Matthew*, Tyndale NT Commentary Series (Downers Grove: Intervarsity, 1985), 202.

31 There are all kinds of theories regarding the precise intent of the letter, the exact identity of the audience, and even who wrote the book. A good place to start with regard to an introduction to the historical scenario in which the book was written is Herman Bateman, IV, ed., *Four Views on the Warning Passages in Hebrews* (Grand Rapids: Kregel, 2007).

32 It is interesting that the AOH uses significantly more space explaining Melchizedek's role in salvation history than the actual space he is given in the brief account in Genesis 14. Though a short story in the OT, he plays an important role as a connection point between the old

covenant and the New.

33 Some interpret this language about Melchizedek to mean that he could not have been a mere human being. Thus, some deduce that he was actually a "Christophany," or the pre-incarnate Christ in human form.

34 Willem A. VanGemeren, *Interpreting the Prophetic Word: An Introduction to the Prophetic Literature of the OT* (Grand Rapids, MI: Zondervan, 1990), 33.

35 P. E. Hughes, "Moses," in *The New Dictionary of Biblical Theology*, eds., T. Desmond Alexander, et al. (Downers Grove: Intervarsity, 2000). 669.

36 Some have speculated that Moses and Elijah appeared to talk to Christ because they discussed his upcoming departure, or *exodon* (exodus). And would be more specialized in divine departures than Moses who led Israel out of Egypt and Elijah who rode a chariot of fire into heaven and escaped death.

37 Luke also mentions the same teachings in his gospel account in 6:20-49. Yet he describes it as occurring on a plain as opposed to a hill or mountain. Scholars debate whether Jesus gave these teachings twice or whether Matthew's account is referring to the same event. If it is, then perhaps Luke is not mentioning all of the exact details that Matthew records.

38 T. Desmond Alexander, *From Eden to New Jerusalem: An Introduction to Biblical Theology* (Grand Rapids, MI: Kregel, 2008), 27-28.

39 There is a major dispute among biblical scholars as to whether these "sons of God" were mortal men who acted immorally or possibly angels who violated their heavenly estate to cohabitate with women. In either case, the point we want to emphasize is that this event was apparently the proverbial straw that broke the camel's back. Once it

occurred, the Lord determined that judgment must fall.

40 T. Desmond Alexander, *From Eden to New Jerusalem: An Introduction to Biblical Theology* (Grand Rapids, MI: Kregel, 2008), 29.

41 M. Turner, "Languages," in the *New Dictionary of Biblical Theology*, eds. T. Desmond Alexander, et al. (Downers Grove: Intervarsity, 2000), 628.

42 Graeme Goldsworthy, *According to the Plan: The Unfolding Revelation of God in the Bible* (Downers Grove: Intervarsity, 1991), 117

43 S. Motyer, "Israel," in the *New Dictionary of Biblical Theology*, 583-584.

44 See a helpful summary of this point in Brant Pitre, "Jesus, the New Temple, and the New Priesthood," *Letter & Spirit* 4 (2008), 56-57.

45 It is because of this dilemma with the initial relationship between the Mosaic and Davidic covenants that the later prophets began to speak of a new covenant. Under the old covenant, the Davidic promise was stalled because of the constant disobedience of Davidic kings and the idolatry of the nation which led to the assortment of Mosaic curses that culminated in exile. The ordeal was that the Law could not change sinful hearts but only regulate and define sin. Therefore, the Lord promised that he would establish a final covenant with His people wherein His law would be written on their hearts, they would be forgiven of their sins, and they would have eternal life and be resurrected from the dead. Likewise, they would be restored nationally and be protected by a leader of integrity (Jer. 31:33-34; Ezek. 11:19-20; 36:25-27; 37:1-23; Dan. 12:1-2). This facet of God's kingdom is critical to the development of salvation in the NT, but space here does not permit further examination.

46 Some of the initial connections highlighted in the rest of this chapter derive from the sermon of a former colleague, Dr. Daniel Streett. His

observations on Deuteronomy 17 and the requirements of Israel's king are invaluable to the development of this chapter.

47 There is a question as to what exactly the king is expected to copy. Is it only Deuteronomy, just the legislative portions that are pertinent to the king, or the whole Torah? See discussion in Peter C. Craigie, *The Book of Deuteronomy*, The New International Commentary on the OT (Grand Rapids: Eerdmans, 1976), 256-257.

48 Jeremy R. Treat, *The Crucified King: Atonement and Kingdom in Biblical and Systematic Theology* (Grand Rapids, MI: Zondervan, 2014), 240-41.

49 In Chapter 7, we examine how Jesus serves as a new temple for God's people.

50 Other examples of leaders riding donkeys as a sign of piece include Jdg. 5:10, 10:4, 12:14, and 2 Sam. 16:2.

51 This does not mean necessarily that the Church is some sort of new covenant version of Israel. Rather, it means that Israel is now defined in terms of those who are in Christ whether one is a Jew or a Gentile. Chapter 5 teases this out more by discussing how Jesus is the true Israel.

52 Timothy Keller, *King's Cross: The Story of the World in the Life of Jesus* (New York, NY: Dutton, 2011), 20.

53 While Adam and Eve being cast out of the Garden was clearly a form of judgment (exile), in another sense it was an act of mercy because Genesis records the Lord as saying that if they ate from the tree of life, they would be in a possibly immortal and unredeemable state (Gen. 3:22-24). Likewise, before sending them away, the Lord also was merciful in providing animal skins to cover their shame (Gen. 3:21).

54 An excellent discussion about these parallels can be found in Michael S. Heiser, *The Unseen Realm* (Bellingham, WA: Lexham Press, 2015), 46-47.

55 For a fantastic discussion and expansion of Adam and Eve as the first priests of the first temple, see T. Desmond Alexander, *From Eden to New Jerusalem: An Introduction to Biblical Theology* (Grand Rapids, MI: Kregel, 2008), 20-31.

56 Again, forgive us for being repetitive here. Broken records do not make for good books. But the truth is, it is almost impossible to discuss the tie between the OT and NT—particularly in light of Jesus—without discussing where the story began. From the first bite of the apple, God begins in one specific way (through Jesus), shown in various types and images, to bring mankind back to himself.

57 See a fuller discussion of this point in G. K. Beale, *The Temple and the Church's Mission* (Downers Grove: IVP Academic, 2004).

58 Heiser, *Unseen Realm*, 44-45. This is possibly why the earlier nations attempted to build the Tower of Babel so they could have a heavenly perspective without a mountain view.

59 R. E. Averbeck, "Tabernacle," in the *Dictionary of the OT Pentateuch*, eds. T. Desmond Alexander and David W. Baker (Downers Grove: Intervarsity, 2003), 809.

60 More in depth discussion of these terms can be found in Ibid., 807-812.

61 Heiser, *The Unseen Realm*, 176. Others suggest that the Israelites were forced to face the west went entering the Tabernacle because it opposed the surrounding sun worshippers who always faced the east when praying or worshipping.

62 Averbeck, "Tabernacle," 817; Gordon Wenham, "Sanctuary Symbolism in the in the Garden of Eden Story," in *Proceedings of the Ninth World Congress of Jewish Studies* (Jerusalem: World Union of Jewish Studies, 1986), 19-24

63 The latter idea of "pollution" refers to the OT concept of uncleanness.

Being ceremonially unclean did not necessarily convey the idea of being morally corrupt. It primarily referred to being contaminated or unfit to come into God's presence. Such uncleanness was indicative of death, decay, or imperfection, not evil actions.

64 Often temple sanctuaries were depicted as having multiple levels. See Brant Pitre, "Jesus, the New Temple, and the New Priesthood," *Letter & Spirit* 4 (2008), 55.

65 David's first attempt to bring the ark to Jerusalem was a disaster because he did not follow the Law's instructions on how to transport it (See 1 Sam. 6:1-11; 1 Chron. 13:1-14).

66 P. P. Jenson, "Temple," in the *Dictionary of the OT Prophets*, eds. Mark J. Boda and J. Gordon McConville (Downers Grove: Intervarsity, 2012), 767.

67 Heiser, *The Unseen Realm*, 224-225.

68 This is not to deny that Israel's hope had more theological components. The most central feature was that it was Messianic to the core.

69 Also, the Father's presence then encompassed the mountain and he spoke in affirmation of his Son's identity.

70 Scripture goes on to extend the theme of Christ as the true temple to his people, the Church. Because he gives the Spirit to them, the divine presence now indwells them, thereby making their bodies individually holy (sacred) and making them a holy people as a whole.

71 Technically, one can make a legitimate distinction between a diary and a journal. But for our purposes in this chapter, we are using these words interchangeably.

72 All of this basic information about the historical background of the Psalms can be found in any good commentary, survey, or Bible dictionary. For those interested in more information, two excellent resources

to consult are Tremper Longman III, *How to Read the Psalms* (Downers Grove: InterVarsity, 1988); and C. Hassell Bullock, *Encountering the Psalms* (Grand Rapids: Baker, 2004).

73 There are all kinds of scholarly debates about the reliability of the authorship of various Psalms. But that area of inquiry is not our concern here. If one is interested in reading a little more about this discussion though, a good place to start is with D. A. Brueggeman, "Psalms 4: Titles," in the *Dictionary of the OT: Wisdom, Poetry & Writings*, eds., Tremper Longman III and Peter Enns (Downers Grove: InterVarsity, 2008), 615-621.

74 All of the categories we mention can be broken down into further sections and others could be added as well as subtracted. We're just wanting to discuss a few themes that are dominant. But good introductions that discuss this topic much further are Rolf A. Jacobson and Karl Jacobson, *Invitation to the Psalms* (Grand Rapids: Baker, 2013); and Tremper Longman III, *How to Read the Psalms* (Downers Grove: InterVarsity, 1988).

75 Again, the link between David as the King of Israel and Christ as his rightful regal heir is discussed in Chapter 6.

76 Later NT writers pick up on this theme and make the point that believers are now living stones that are connected to Christ and forming a kind of organic temple (see Eph 2:20-21; 1 Pet 2:4-5).

77 Also, while they are not directly quoted, the metaphors that David used to describe his desperate state are remarkably transformed into literal details that Jesus experienced while on the cross; e.g., pierced hands and feet, dry mouth needing something to drink, and bones being out of joint.

78 As we read on, we still see Jesus entrusting himself to his Father at his death by quoting Psalm 31:5. This Psalm opens with David professing

his confidence in the Lord's care. So much so that he was willing to commit his spirit, or life, to him. In like manner, Jesus prays this confession with his dying breath (Lk 23:46). And interestingly enough, David's despair in Psalm 22, which Jesus is replicating, is tempered by his hope that the Lord will not hide his face forever. He will hear David's cries for help (Ps 22:24). This is probably part of the reason why the early church made a parallel between Psalm 16 and Christ's resurrection. Here, just as King David knew the Lord would not let death defeat him, so the Father did not let the grave defeat Christ after he was crucified (cf., Ps 16:9-10; Acts 2:26-27).

79 The significance of the comment about Melchizedek is covered in more detail in chapter three.

80 There are several views as to who David was referring to when he wrote the Psalm. Our point here is that Jesus interprets the Psalm as referring to himself. For a survey of views on this Psalm, you can read an article by John Aloisi, "Who is David's Lord? Another Look at Psalm 110:1," *Detroit Biblical Seminary Journal* 10 (2005), 103-123.

81 For an interesting discussion on this Psalm and others as an eternal conversation between God the Father and the God the Son, check out Matthew W. Bates, *The Birth of the Trinity* (Oxford: Oxford University Press, 2015).

82 There are other Psalms referenced in the Gospels about Jesus or used by him that we did not cover; e.g., 6:3; 8:2; 34:20; 62:12; 78:2; 82:6; 118:22-23.

83 Eugene Merrill, "The Sign of Jonah," *Journal of the Evangelical Theological Society* 23, no. 1 (1980), 27.

84 John Woodhouse, "Jesus and Jonah," *Reformed Theological Review* XLIII, no. 2 (1984), 33.

85 Any pastor can relate to this.

86 Another obvious point is that Jonah was reluctant to follow God's call; the disciples dropped everything to follow Jesus.

87 Jesus is described as making the same claims again in Matthew 16:1-4. The only difference is that he doesn't even explain the sign at all. He simply says it's the only one left for the unbelieving Jewish leaders to expect.

88 T. Desmond Alexander, "Jonah," in the *New Dictionary of Biblical Theology*, eds., T. Desmond Alexander, et al. (Downers Grove: Intervarsity, 2000), 605-606.

89 John Nolland describes it this way: "To Jonah's surprise (and consternation) the Ninevites repented at his preaching. The unspoken point is that Jesus's generation has not repented at his preaching, and this despite the fact that ... they are experiencing something greater than what was available to the Ninevites," in *The Gospel of Matthew: A Commentary on the Greek Text* (Grand Rapids, MI: Eerdmans, 2005), 512.

90 Herman Bavinck, *Reformed Dogmatics*, vol. 1 (Grand Rapids, MI: Baker Academic, 2003), 394-97.

ABOUT THE AUTHORS

Brandon D. Smith (Ph.D. Candidate, Ridley College) works with the Christian Standard Bible and is an editor for Holman Bible Publishers. He also serves as Editorial Director for the Center for Baptist Renewal and is the co-author of *Rooted: Theology for Growing Christians*.

Everett Berry is Professor of Theology at Criswell College and Editor of the *Criswell Theological Review*. He has written for several publications, including the *Southern Baptist Journal of Theology* and the *Westminster Theological Journal*. He and his family live near Dallas, Texas.

Made in the USA
Middletown, DE
04 September 2019